Java™ Design Pattern

Essentials

-

Second Edition

Java™ Design Pattern

Essentials

-

Second Edition

Tony Bevis

Ability First Limited
Essex, United Kingdom

AbilityFIRST

Java Design Pattern Essentials – Second Edition

British Library Cataloguing in Publication Data. A catalogue record for this book is available from the British Library.

Publishing history:

- First edition, May 2010 (ISBN 978-0-9565758-0-7)

- Second edition, October 2012

Published by:

Ability First Limited

Dragon Enterprise Centre, 28 Stephenson Road

Leigh-on-Sea, Essex SS9 5LY, United Kingdom

www.abilityfirst.co.uk/books

ISBN: 978-0-9565758-4-5

Cover image by Ivan Polushkin, copyright Fotolia.

This book is dedicated to

"The Gang of Four"

Table of Contents

Preface

This book is an introductory guide to the world of object-oriented software design patterns. The examples and code extracts have been deliberately kept simple, allowing you to concentrate on understanding the concepts and application of each pattern rather than having to wade through irrelevant source code.

The book assumes that you have at least a basic knowledge of the Java programming language, including understanding what is meant by the terms encapsulation, inheritance and polymorphism, and that you know how to write classes and interfaces. By the end of this book you should be able to apply that knowledge to the design of complex applications, where objects from multiple classes need to interact to accomplish particular goals.

The patterns described within comprise all 23 of the patterns in the seminal work of Erich Gamma, Richard Helm, Ralph Johnson and John Vlissides; *Design Patterns: Elements of Reusable Object-Oriented Software* (Addison-Wesley, 1995). There are also four additional patterns described including Model-View-Controller (MVC), now a mainstay of graphical applications. For the most part, each chapter is self-contained, and you can therefore dip into the patterns in any order. However, it is recommended that you read Chapter 1 *"What are Design Patterns?"* first to familiarise yourself with the common theme and the object-oriented principles that the patterns utilise.

This book also makes use of a simplified implementation of Unified Modeling Language (UML) diagrams to show how the classes that comprise a pattern are structured. If you are unfamiliar with UML diagrams then you may wish to refer to Appendix A before you begin.

Prerequisite knowledge

In order to make use of this book you should have a basic understanding of both the Java language and of object-oriented principles. In particular, you should know how to create classes, interfaces and enums, and understand the terms encapsulation, inheritance, composition and polymorphism.

How this book is organised

Part I introduces the idea of design patterns, and lays the foundation for some simple core classes that comprise the common theme used throughout this book.

Part II describes the five creational patterns, that is, those that help manage the instantiation of objects.

Part III describes the seven structural patterns, that is, those that help manage how classes are organised and interrelate.

Part IV describes the eleven behavioural patterns, that is, those that help manage what the classes actually do.

Part V describes four additional patterns you should find useful in practical applications.

Part VI contains a single chapter that develops a simple 3-tier application that uses some of the more commonly used design patterns.

Part VII contains the appendixes, which includes a brief explanation of the Unified Modeling Language (UML) diagram formats for those unfamiliar with UML, and a quick reference for each of the 23 main patterns.

Conventions used in this book

Java code that you need to enter, or results that are shown as output, is shown in a fixed-width font as follows:

```
anObject.doSomething();
anotherObject.doThis();
```

Often, a piece of additional or modified code is provided, and the parts that are new or changed are indicated in **bold**:

```
anObject.doSomethingElseInstead();
anObject.alsoDoThis();
anotherObject.doThis();
```

Names of classes, objects or Java statements will appear in the text using a fixed-width font such as `MyClass` or `someObject`, for example.

Where some useful or important additional information about a topic is included it will be shown in a note-box, like the following:

This is some additional information in a note-box.

For reasons of brevity, `package` and `import` statements are omitted from most of the code samples in this book.

The book's resources

You can also download all of the Java source code from this book from our website:

http://www.abilityfirst.co.uk/books

Preface to the Second Edition

This fully revised and updated second edition was borne out of receiving several positive reviews and helpful feedback from readers of the first edition of this book. Wherever possible, the code has been made more straightforward and the text more clear, and as such there are changes in most of the chapters of this book. The opportunity was also taken to update the formatting of the book and to redraw the UML diagrams.

The chapter describing the *Singleton* pattern has been updated to demonstrate both the "traditional" approach and Java's useful `enum` facility, which simplifies the coding of thread-safe singletons. The chapters on *Flyweight* and *Proxy* have also been updated to use easier to follow examples.

This edition also now includes the *Layers* pattern, and more significantly there is an additional chapter showing how to combine several patterns together into a simple 3-tier graphical application.

I am extremely grateful to the following for their feedback and suggestions which I hope will make this edition an improvement upon the previous one: Dr. Carl Evans, Donie O'Brien, Randolf Rothfuss and Geoff Cater.

September 2012.

Part I.   Introduction

This part introduces the idea of design patterns, and lays the foundation for some simple core classes that comprise the common theme used throughout this book.

1. What are Design Patterns?

Imagine that you have just been assigned the task of designing a software system. Your customer tells you that he needs to model the Gadgets his factory makes and that each Gadget comprises the same component parts but those parts are a bit different for each type of Gadget. And he also makes Gizmos, where each Gizmo comes with a selection of optional extras any combination of which can be chosen. And he also needs a unique sequential serial number stamped on each item made.

Just how would you go about designing these classes?

The chances are that no matter what problem domain you are working in, somebody else has had to design a similar solution in the past. Not necessarily for Gadgets and Gizmos of course, but conceptually similar in terms of objectives and structure. In other words there's a good chance that a generic solution or approach already exists, and all you need to do is to apply that approach to solve your design conundrum.

This is what *Design Patterns* are for. They describe generic solutions to software design problems. Once versed in patterns, you might think to yourself "those Gadgets could be modelled using the *Abstract Factory* pattern, the Gizmos using the *Decorator* pattern, and the serial number generation using the *Singleton* pattern."

How this book uses patterns

This book gives worked examples for each of the 23 patterns described in the classic reference work *Design Patterns – Elements of Reusable Object-Oriented Software* (Gamma, 1995) plus four additional useful patterns, including Model-View-Controller (MVC).

Each of the worked examples in this book uses a common theme drawn from the business world, being that of a fictional vehicle manufacturer called the Foobar Motor Company. The company makes a range of cars and vans together with the engines used to power the vehicles. You should therefore familiarise yourself with the classes described in this introduction.

The class hierarchy looks like this:

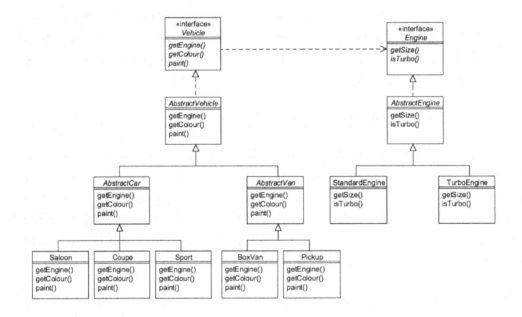

Figure 1.1 : Vehicle and Engine class hierarchies

Vehicle and Engine are the root interfaces of the hierarchies, with each vehicle object requiring a reference to an Engine object. AbstractVehicle is an abstract class that implements the Vehicle interface, and AbstractEngine likewise implements the Engine interface. For vehicles, we also have AbstractCar and AbstractVan together with concrete subclassses Saloon, Coupe and Sport as types of cars. AbstractVan has the concrete subclasses BoxVan and Pickup as types of van.

The concrete subclasses of AbstractEngine are StandardEngine and TurboEngine.

Despite there being several classes in the hierarchies the code for each has been kept deliberately simple so you can focus on understanding the patterns rather than having to decipher complex code. To illustrate this, here is the Java source code for the Engine interface:

```
public interface Engine {

    public int getSize();
    public boolean isTurbo();

}
```

This simple interface merely requires method getters to return the engine size (in cubic centimetres) and whether it is turbocharged.

The AbstractEngine class looks like this:

```
public abstract class AbstractEngine implements Engine {

    private int size;
    private boolean turbo;

    public AbstractEngine(int size, boolean turbo) {
        this.size = size;
        this.turbo = turbo;
    }

    public int getSize() {
        return size;
    }

    public boolean isTurbo() {
        return turbo;
    }

    public String toString() {
        return getClass().getSimpleName() +
                " (" + size + ")";
    }

}
```

This simplified implementation of an engine requires the appropriate attributes to be supplied in the constructor. The `toString()` method has been implemented to produce output in this format:

```
StandardEngine (1300)
TurboEngine (2000)
```

The `equals()` and `hashCode()` methods will inherit from `Object` and therefore use object identity. This makes sense, since for example, two separate 1300cc Standard Engines are logically different entities and so should be treated as such (one engine would go into one vehicle and the other engine into a different vehicle).

The concrete subclasses are trivially simple:

```java
public class StandardEngine extends AbstractEngine {

    public StandardEngine(int size) {
        super(size, false); // not turbocharged
    }

}


public class TurboEngine extends AbstractEngine {

    public TurboEngine(int size) {
        super(size, true); // turbocharged
    }

}
```

Now that you have seen the `Engine` hierarchy we can look at the `Vehicle` interface:

```java
public interface Vehicle {

    public enum Colour {UNPAINTED, BLUE, BLACK, GREEN,
                        RED, SILVER, WHITE, YELLOW};

    public Engine getEngine();
    public Vehicle.Colour getColour();
    public void paint(Vehicle.Colour colour);

}
```

A nested `enum` called `Colour` defines the possible colours that each `Vehicle` object could be.

This is how the `AbstractVehicle` class implements `Vehicle`:

```
public abstract class AbstractVehicle implements Vehicle {

    private Engine engine;
    private Vehicle.Colour colour;

    public AbstractVehicle(Engine engine) {
        this(engine, Vehicle.Colour.UNPAINTED);
    }

    public AbstractVehicle(Engine engine, Vehicle.Colour colour) {
        this.engine = engine;
        this.colour = colour;
    }

    public Engine getEngine() {
        return engine;
    }

    public Vehicle.Colour getColour() {
        return colour;
    }

    public void paint(Vehicle.Colour colour) {
        this.colour = colour;
    }

    public String toString() {
        return getClass().getSimpleName() +
                " (" + engine + ", " + colour + ")";
    }

}
```

The overloaded constructors in `AbstractVehicle` require an `Engine` object and optionally a vehicle colour to be supplied.

The output of calls to `toString()` will be in this format:

```
Saloon (StandardEngine (1300), RED)
BoxVan (TurboEngine (2200), WHITE)
```

The `AbstractCar` and `AbstractVan` classes just forward to the constructors (obviously real classes would define whatever is different between cars and vans):

```
public abstract class AbstractCar extends AbstractVehicle {

    public AbstractCar(Engine engine) {
        this(engine, Vehicle.Colour.UNPAINTED)
    }

    public AbstractCar(Engine engine, Vehicle.Colour colour) {
        super(engine, colour);
    }

}



public abstract class AbstractVan extends AbstractVehicle {

    public AbstractVan(Engine engine) {
        this(engine, Vehicle.Colour.UNPAINTED)
    }

    public AbstractVan(Engine engine, Vehicle.Colour colour) {
        super(engine, colour);
    }
}
```

The concrete subclasses also just forward to the constructors:

```
public class Saloon extends AbstractCar {

    public Saloon(Engine engine) {
        this(engine, Vehicle.Colour.UNPAINTED)
    }

    public Saloon(Engine engine, Vehicle.Colour colour) {
        super(engine, colour);
    }

}



public class Coupe extends AbstractCar {

    public Coupe(Engine engine) {
        this(engine, Vehicle.Colour.UNPAINTED)
    }

    public Coupe(Engine engine, Vehicle.Colour colour) {
        super(engine, colour);
```

```
        }

    }


public class Sport extends AbstractCar {

    public Sport(Engine engine) {
        this(engine, Vehicle.Colour.UNPAINTED)
    }

    public Sport(Engine engine, Vehicle.Colour colour) {
        super(engine, colour);
    }

}


public class BoxVan extends AbstractVan {

    public BoxVan(Engine engine) {
        this(engine, Vehicle.Colour.UNPAINTED)
    }

    public BoxVan(Engine engine, Vehicle.Colour colour) {
        super(engine, colour);
    }

}


public class Pickup extends AbstractVan {

    public Pickup(Engine engine) {
        this(engine, Vehicle.Colour.UNPAINTED)
    }

    public Pickup(Engine engine, Vehicle.Colour colour) {
        super(engine, colour);
    }

}
```

Many of the patterns in this book utilise one or more of the above classes in some way, often adding additional functionality or classes for the purposes of explaining the pattern in question. You will also frequently see reference to a Client class; this just refers to whatever class is making use of the pattern under discussion.

How patterns are categorised

Each of the patterns described in this book fall under one of three categories; *Creational, Structural* or *Behavioural*:

- *Creational* patterns provide approaches to object instantiation. Where you place the `new` keyword affects how tightly or loosely coupled your classes are;

- *Structural* patterns provide approaches for combining classes and objects to form larger structures. Deciding whether to use inheritance or composition affects how flexible and adaptable your software is;

- *Behavioural* patterns provide approaches for handling communication between objects.

Common principles in design patterns

Experience has shown that some object-oriented approaches are more flexible than others. Here is a summary of the main principles that the patterns in this book strive to adhere to:

1. ***Program to an interface, not an implementation.*** By "interface" is meant the general concept of abstraction, which could refer to a Java interface or an abstract class. To accomplish this, use the most general type (e.g. interface) possible when declaring variables, constructor and method arguments, etc. Doing so gives extra flexibility as to the actual types that are used at run-time.

2. ***Prefer object composition over inheritance.*** Where a class is related to another in some way, you should distinguish between "is a" (or "is a type of") and "has a" relationships. In the `Vehicle` and `Engine` hierarchies described earlier, it is true to say that `AbstractCar` "is a" `Vehicle`, and that `Saloon` "is a" `AbstractCar`. But it would not be true to say that `Vehicle` "is a" `Engine`, but rather that a `Vehicle` "has a"

`Engine`. Therefore, inheritance is legitimately used for `AbstractCar` and `Saloon`, but object composition is used between `Vehicle` and `Engine`. Do not be tempted to use inheritance just to save having to write some methods. Sometimes using a "has a" relationship is more flexible even when an "is a" relationship seems the natural choice. You will see an example of this in the *Decorator* pattern.

3. ***Keep objects loosely-coupled.*** Ideally, classes should model just one thing, and only be composed of other objects that are genuinely required (such as a `Vehicle` requiring an `Engine`). Ask yourself what would happen if you wanted to use a class you have written in a completely different application; what "baggage" (i.e. other classes) would also need to be copied? By keeping this to a minimum, you make your class more re-usable. A good example of a pattern that uses loose-coupling is *Observer*.

4. ***Encapsulate the concept that varies.*** If you've written a class in which some parts are the same for each instance but another part of the class varies for each instance, consider extracting the latter into a class of its own, which is referenced by the original class. An example pattern that uses principle is *Strategy*.

Some general advice

The principles listed above will become more apparent as we explore the patterns in detail. You should also note that the patterns described in this book give a general approach to a particular problem. It is quite acceptable for you to modify or adapt them to better fit your particular problem. And it is very common for multiple patterns to be combined to solve complex problems.

However, do remember that you should strive to keep things simple. It is easy, after reading a book such as this, to think that you have to find a pattern to solve a particular problem when an even simpler solution might be available. One of the mantras of Extreme Programming (XP) is "You aren't going to need it", the idea being that you should avoid adding features before they are required, and this philosophy could also be applied to patterns – beware of adding an unnecessary feature just so you can apply a pattern. Patterns are not a "magic bullet", just another set of tools in your toolkit, albeit an indispensable set.

Use your knowledge and experience to judge whether a pattern should be applied to your circumstances, and if so to what extent you need to adapt it. A good example of when applying patterns may be beneficial is when you are "refactoring" existing code. Refactoring is when you are changing the structure of some software but not its behaviour, to improve its maintainability and flexibility. This provides a good opportunity to examine your code to see if a pattern might provide a better structure, such as replacing conditionals, or defining factory classes to aid object instantiation.

Patterns have been applied to many programming languages besides Java, particularly object-oriented languages, and indeed other fields, having originated by being applied to architectural design. And new patterns are being developed and applied on a regular basis, so you may view this book as merely a starting point in the subject.

Part II. Creational Patterns

This part describes the five creational patterns, that is, those that help manage the instantiation of objects.

- *Abstract Factory*: Provide an interface for creating families of related or dependent objects without specifying their concrete classes;

- *Builder*: Separate the construction of a complex object from its representation so that the same construction process can create different representations;

- *Factory Method*: Define an interface for creating an object, but let subclasses decide which class to instantiate;

- *Prototype*: Specify the kinds of objects to create using a prototypical instance, and create new objects by copying the prototype;

- *Singleton*: Ensure a class allows only one object to be created, providing a single point of access to it.

2. Abstract Factory

Type	Creational
Purpose	Provide an interface for creating families of related or dependent objects without specifying their concrete classes.

The Foobar Motor Company makes cars and vans, which when being built comprises (among lots of other things) a body shell, a chassis and glassware for the windows. Although both cars and vans need all of the same types of components, the specifics of each type differ depending upon whether it is being used for a car or a van.

In other words:

- *A car's body shell is different from a van's body shell;*

- *A car's chassis is different from a van's chassis;*

- *A car's windows are different from a van's windows.*

Therefore, when we need to build a vehicle we can think of the components as coming from different 'families'; that is, when we build a car we use one family of components and when we build a van we use a different family of components.

We can thus model the components into simple hierarchies, as illustrated in the following figure:

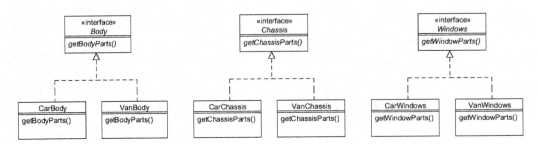

Figure 2.1 : Body, Chassis & Windows class hierarchies

As you can see, there is an interface for `Body` having implementations of `CarBody` and `VanBody`. Likewise we have similar separate hierarchies for `Chassis` and `Windows`.

The code for the `Body` hierarchy is very simple:

```
public interface Body {

    public String getBodyParts();

}


public class CarBody implements Body {

    public String getBodyParts() {
        return "Body shell parts for a car";
    }

}


public class VanBody implements Body {

    public String getBodyParts() {
        return "Body shell parts for a van";
    }

}
```

The code for the `Chassis` hierarchy is almost identical:

```
public interface Chassis {

    public String getChassisParts();

}
```

```
public class CarChassis implements Chassis {

    public String getChassisParts() {
        return "Chassis parts for a car";
    }

}
```

```
public class VanChassis implements Chassis {

    public String getChassisParts() {
        return "Chassis parts for a van";
    }

}
```

And likewise the code for the `Windows` **hierarchy:**

```
public interface Windows {

    public String getWindowParts();

}
```

```
public class CarWindows implements Windows {

    public String getWindowParts() {
        return "Window glassware for a car";
    }

}
```

```
public class VanWindows implements Windows {

    public String getWindowParts() {
        return "Window glassware for a van";
    }

}
```

Now we need a way of getting the correct family of parts (either for a car or for a van) but without having to explicitly instantiate the specific type in client programs each time we require them. To accomplish this, we shall define "factory" classes that will do this for us:

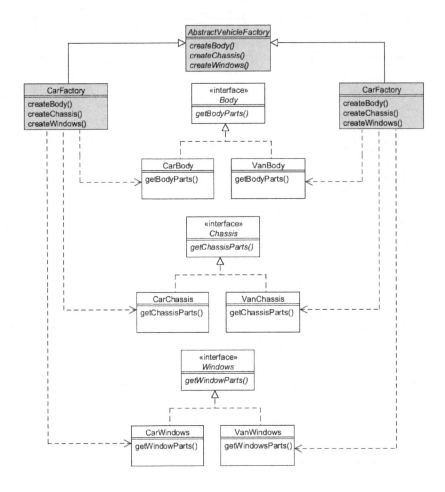

Figure 2.2 : Abstract Factory pattern

The `AbstractVehicleFactory` class is an abstract class that defines the abstract methods `createBody()`, `createChassis()` and `createWindows()`, returning a `Body`, `Chassis` and `Windows` object respectively:

```
public abstract class AbstractVehicleFactory {
```

```
    public abstract Body createBody();
    public abstract Chassis createChassis();
    public abstract Windows createWindows();

}
```

The concrete subclass `CarFactory` returns the objects specific for the `Car` family:

```
public class CarFactory extends AbstractVehicleFactory {

    public Body createBody() {
        return new CarBody();
    }

    public Chassis createChassis() {
        return new CarChassis();
    }

    public Windows createWindows() {
        return new CarWindows();
    }
}
```

The concrete subclass `VanFactory` returns the objects specific for the `Van` family:

```
public class VanFactory extends AbstractVehicleFactory {

    public Body createBody() {
        return new VanBody();
    }

    public Chassis createChassis() {
        return new VanChassis();
    }

    public Windows createWindows() {
        return new VanWindows();
    }
}
```

Now it just remains for client programs to instantiate the appropriate 'factory' after which it can obtain the correct parts without having to specify whether they are for a car or a van:

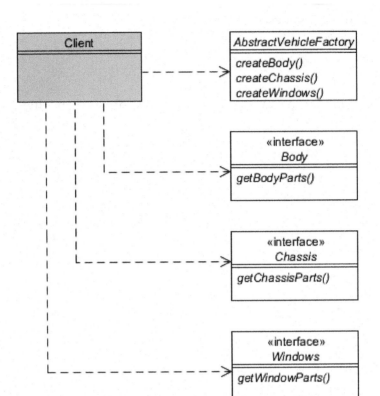

Figure 2.3 : How clients use Abstract Factory

```
String whatToMake = "car"; // or "van"

AbstractVehicleFactory factory = null;

// Create the correct 'factory'...
if (whatToMake.equals("car")) {
    factory = new CarFactory();
} else {
    factory = new VanFactory();
}

// Create the vehicle's component parts...
// These will either be all car parts or all van parts.
Body vehicleBody = factory.createBody();
Chassis vehicleChassis = factory.createChassis();
Windows vehicleWindows = factory.createWindows();

// Show what we've created...
System.out.println(vehicleBody.getBodyParts());
```

```
System.out.println(vehicleChassis.getChassisParts());
System.out.println(vehicleWindows.getWindowParts());
```

Therefore your client program needs to know if it is making a car or a van, but once it has instantiated the correct factory all the methods to create the parts can be done using an identical set of method calls.

The main disadvantage of the *Abstract Factory* pattern arises if you need to add additional 'products'. For example, if we now need to include `Lights` in the family of components, we would need to amend `AbstractVehicleFactory`, `CarFactory` and `VanFactory`, in addition to creating a new `Lights` hierarchy (`CarLights` and `VanLights`).

3. Builder

Type	Creational
Purpose	Separate the construction of a complex object from its representation so that the same construction process can create different representations.

The Foobar Motor Company makes cars and vans, and the construction process of each differs in detail; for example, the body shell of a van comprises a cab area and a large reinforced storage area, whereas a saloon car comprises a passenger area and a luggage area (i.e. boot). And of course there a number of complex steps that have to be undertaken regardless of what type of vehicle is being built.

The *Builder* pattern facilitates the construction of complex objects by separating the individual steps into separate methods in a *Builder* hierarchy, and then using a *Director* object to specify the required steps in the correct order. Finally, the finished product is retrieved from the *Builder*.

The following diagram shows these relationships:

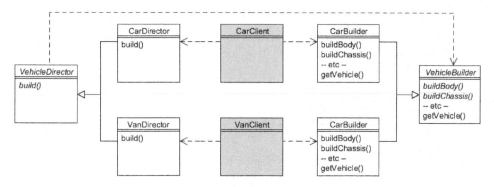

Figure 3.1 : Builder pattern

We start off with the abstract `VehicleBuilder` class:

```
public abstract class VehicleBuilder {

    public void buildBody() {}
    public void buildBoot() {}
    public void buildChassis() {}
    public void buildPassengerArea() {}
    public void buildReinforcedStorageArea() {}
    public void buildWindows() {}

    public abstract Vehicle getVehicle();

}
```

Note how this class defines all possible 'build' methods for both cars and vans, and provides empty implementations for each as a default. The abstract `getVehicle()` method is for returning the finished vehicle.

The `CarBuilder` class inherits from `VehicleBuilder` and overrides the appropriate methods:

```
public class CarBuilder extends VehicleBuilder {

    private AbstractCar carInProgress;

    public CarBuilder(AbstractCar car) {
        carInProgress = car;
    }

    public void buildBody() {
        // Add body to carInProgress
        System.out.println("building car body");
    }

    public void buildBoot() {
        // Add boot to carInProgress
        System.out.println("building car boot");
    }

    public void buildChassis() {
        // Add chassis to carInProgress
        System.out.println("building car chassis");
    }

    public void buildPassengerArea() {
        // Add passenger area to carInProgress
        System.out.println("building car passenger area");
    }

    public void buildWindows() {
```

```
        // Add windows to carInProgress
        System.out.println("building car windows");
    }

    public Vehicle getVehicle() {
        return carInProgress;
    }

}
```

Note that the `buildReinforcedStorageArea()` method was not overridden since it is not applicable to cars.

The `VanBuilder` class overrides the appropriate methods to build a van:

```
public class VanBuilder extends VehicleBuilder {

    private AbstractVan vanInProgress;

    public VanBuilder(AbstractVan van) {
        vanInProgress = van;
    }

    public void buildBody() {
        // Add body to vanInProgress
        System.out.println("building van body");
    }

    public void buildChassis() {
        // Add chassis to vanInProgress
        System.out.println("building van chassis");
    }

    public void buildReinforcedStorageArea() {
        // Add storage area to vanInProgress
        System.out.println("building van storage area");
    }

    public void buildWindows() {
        // Add windows to vanInProgress
        System.out.println("building van windows");
    }

    public Vehicle getVehicle() {
        return vanInProgress;
    }

}
```

Note that the buildBoot() and buildPassengerArea() methods were not overridden since they are not applicable to vans.

The VehicleDirector abstract class requires a VehicleBuilder object passed to its build() method for implementation by subclasses:

```
public abstract class VehicleDirector {

    public abstract Vehicle build(VehicleBuilder builder);

}
```

The CarDirector class inherits from VehicleDirector and provides the step-by-step process for building a car:

```
public class CarDirector extends VehicleDirector {

    public Vehicle build(VehicleBuilder builder) {
        builder.buildChassis();
        builder.buildBody();
        builder.buildPassengerArea();
        builder.buildBoot();
        builder.buildWindows();
        return builder.getVehicle();
    }

}
```

The VanDirector class provides the step-by-step process for building a van:

```
public class VanDirector extends VehicleDirector {

    public Vehicle build(VehicleBuilder builder) {
        builder.buildChassis();
        builder.buildBody();
        builder.buildReinforcedStorageArea();
        builder.buildWindows();
        return builder.getVehicle();
    }

}
```

As an example of how to use the above classes, let's assume we want to build a `Saloon` car:

```
AbstractCar car = new Saloon(new StandardEngine(1300));
VehicleBuilder builder = new CarBuilder(car);
VehicleDirector director = new CarDirector();
Vehicle v = director.build(builder);
System.out.println(v);
```

You can see the required *Builder* object is constructed and passed to the required *Director* object, after which we invoke the method to build the product and then retrieve the finished article. The output should show:

```
Building car chassis
Building car body
Building car passenger area
Building car boot
Building car windows
Saloon (StandardEngine (1300), UNPAINTED)
```

4. Factory Method

Type	Creational
Purpose	Define an interface for creating an object, but let subclasses decide which class to instantiate.

You will recall from the introduction the following class hierarchy for the vehicles made by the Foobar Motor Company:

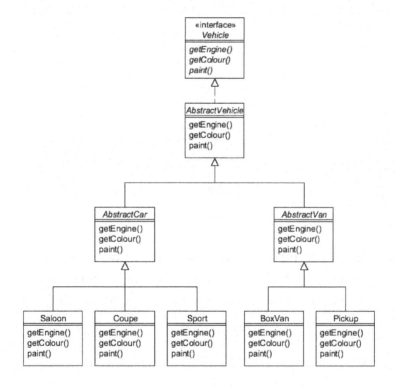

Figure 4.1 : Vehicle class hierarchy

When we need to instantiate a particular type of vehicle (such as a Coupe) it is often more flexible to define a separate class whose responsibility it is to manage the instantiation. This separate class is known as a *Factory*.

The *Factory Method* pattern defines an abstract class which serves as the 'factory' and that has an abstract method within to determine what product (in our case vehicle) to instantiate. Concrete subclasses of the factory make that determination. Here is how the *Factory Method* pattern could be used with the `Vehicle` class hierarchy:

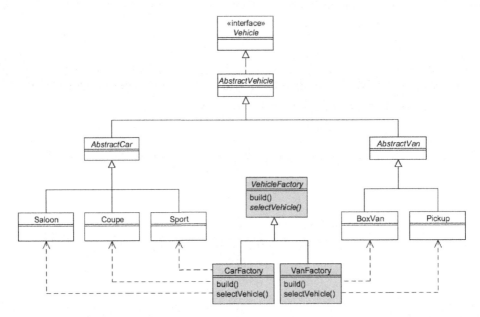

Figure 4.2 : Factory Method pattern

In the above diagram we can see that we have created an abstract `VehicleFactory` class which has two concrete subclasses, `CarFactory` and `VanFactory`. Let us look at how `VehicleFactory` is defined:

```
public abstract class VehicleFactory {

    public enum DrivingStyle {ECONOMICAL, MIDRANGE, POWERFUL};

    public Vehicle build(DrivingStyle style, Vehicle.Colour colour) {
        Vehicle v = selectVehicle(style);
        v.paint(colour);
        return v;
    }

    // This is the "factory method"
    protected abstract Vehicle selectVehicle(DrivingStyle style);

}
```

VehicleFactory contains the public method build() that takes as arguments the driving style (economical, midrange or powerful[1]) and the colour that the vehicle should be painted. The build() method calls the protected abstract selectVehicle() method, which is the "factory method" after which the pattern is named. The implementation of selectVehicle() is therefore delegated to the subclasses such that each subclass determines the specific type of vehicle to instantiate. The method is protected because we only want subclasses to utilise it – it is not intended to be invoked by clients.

Here is the CarFactory concrete subclass:

```
public class CarFactory extends VehicleFactory {

    protected Vehicle selectVehicle(DrivingStyle style) {
        if (style == DrivingStyle.ECONOMICAL) {
            return new Saloon(new StandardEngine(1300));

        } else if (style == DrivingStyle.MIDRANGE) {
            return new Coupe(new StandardEngine(1600));

        } else {
            return new Sport(new TurboEngine(2000));
        }
    }

}
```

As you can see, the selectVehicle() method is implemented such that it works out from the supplied arguments exactly which type of car should be instantiated and returned.

The VanFactory is similar, using the argument to decide which van to instantiate and return:

```
public class VanFactory extends VehicleFactory {

    protected Vehicle selectVehicle(DrivingStyle style) {
        if ((style == DrivingStyle.ECONOMICAL) ||
            (style == DrivingStyle.MIDRANGE)) {
            return new Pickup(new StandardEngine(2200));

        } else {
```

---

[1] Defined as contants in the DrivingStyle enum.

```
                    return new BoxVan(new TurboEngine(2500));
            }
        }

    }
```

Client programs instantiate the required factory and call its `build()` method:

```
// I want an economical car, coloured blue...
VehicleFactory carFactory = new CarFactory();
Vehicle car = carFactory.build
                  (VehicleFactory.DrivingStyle.ECONOMICAL,
                   Vehicle.Colour.BLUE);
System.out.println(car);

// I am a "white van man"...
VehicleFactory vanFactory = new VanFactory();
Vehicle van = vanFactory.build
                  (VehicleFactory.DrivingStyle.POWERFUL,
                   Vehicle.Colour.WHITE);
System.out.println(van);
```

You should see the following output:

```
Saloon (StandardEngine (1300), BLUE)
BoxVan (TurboEngine(2500), WHITE)
```

Using 'static' factory methods

A common and useful variation is to define a `static` factory method. Let's assume we define the following additional `enum` in the `VehicleFactory` class:

```
public enum Category {CAR, VAN};
```

Now we can define the following static `make()` method also in `VehicleFactory` that works out which subclass to instantiate:

```
public static Vehicle make(Category category,
                           DrivingStyle style,
                           Vehicle.Colour colour) {
```

```
        VehicleFactory factory = null;

        if (category == Category.CAR) {
            factory = new CarFactory();

        } else {
            factory = new VanFactory();
        }

        return factory.build(style, colour);
    }
```

Using the `static make()` method is very straightforward:

```
// Create a red sports car...
Vehicle sporty = VehicleFactory.make
                     (VehicleFactory.Category.CAR,
                      VehicleFactory.DrivingStyle.POWERFUL,
                      Colour.RED);
System.out.println(sporty);
```

This should give the following output:

```
Sport (TurboEngine (2000), RED)
```

5. Prototype

Type	Creational
Purpose	Specify the kinds of objects to create using a prototypical instance, and create new objects by copying the prototype.

We shall assume in this chapter that instantiating car and van objects is a time-consuming process, and we therefore need to find a way of speeding up instantiation time whenever we need a new vehicle object.

Here is a reminder of the Vehicle class hierarchy:

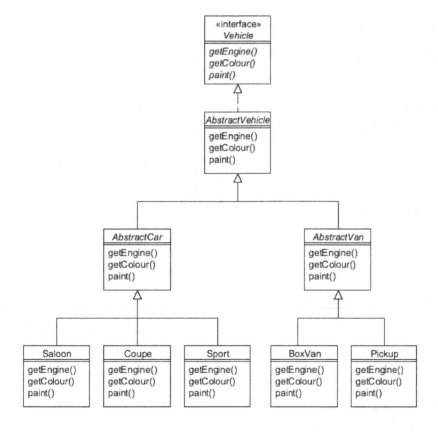

Figure 5.1 : Vehicle class hierarchy

One approach that may improve instantiation time is to utilise Java's `clone()` method. We will therefore specify that the `Vehicle` interface extends `Cloneable` and define the method `clone()`. Code to perform the cloning will then be defined in `AbstractVehicle`. This chapter thus uses a modified version of the `Vehicle` interface and `AbstractVehicle` class as listed below, where the additional code is indicated in bold:

```
public interface Vehicle extends Cloneable {

    public enum Colour {UNPAINTED, BLUE, BLACK, GREEN,
                        RED, SILVER, WHITE, YELLOW};

    public Engine getEngine();
    public Vehicle.Colour getColour();
    public void paint(Vehicle.Colour colour);

    public Object clone();

}


public abstract class AbstractVehicle implements Vehicle {

    private Engine engine;
    private Vehicle.Colour colour;

    public AbstractVehicle(Engine engine) {
        this(engine, Vehicle.Colour.UNPAINTED);
    }

    public AbstractVehicle(Engine engine, Vehicle.Colour colour) {
        this.engine = engine;
        this.colour = colour;
        // ... followed by lots of time-consuming stuff
    }

    public Engine getEngine() {
        return engine;
    }

    public Vehicle.Colour getColour() {
        return colour;
    }

    public void paint(Vehicle.Colour colour) {
        this.colour = colour;
    }

    public Object clone() {
        Object obj = null;
        try {
            obj = super.clone();
```

```
        } catch (CloneNotSupportedException x) {
            // Should not happen...
        }
        return obj;
    }

    public String toString() {
        return getClass().getSimpleName() +
                " (" + engine + ", " + colour + ")";
    }

}
```

The overriding `clone()` method has been made `public`[1] to more easily enable usage by other objects.

None of the car or van subclasses needs to change since they inherit from `Vehicle` at the root of the hierarchy.

We will now define a `VehicleManager` class that will create the initial vehicles from which we can obtain clones:

```
public class VehicleManager {

    private Vehicle saloon, coupe, sport, boxVan, pickup;

    public VehicleManager() {
        // For simplicity all vehicles use same engine type...
        saloon = new Saloon(new StandardEngine(1300));
        coupe = new Coupe(new StandardEngine(1300));
        sport = new Sport(new StandardEngine(1300));
        boxVan = new BoxVan(new StandardEngine(1300));
        pickup = new Pickup(new StandardEngine(1300));
    }

    public Vehicle createSaloon() {
        return (Vehicle) saloon.clone();
    }

    public Vehicle createCoupe() {
        return (Vehicle) coupe.clone();
    }

    public Vehicle createSport() {
        return (Vehicle) sport.clone();
    }

    public Vehicle createBoxVan() {
        return (Vehicle) boxVan.clone();
```

---

[1]The `Object` class defines `clone()` as protected.

```
        }

    public Vehicle createPickup() {
        return (Vehicle) pickup.clone();
    }

}
```

Client programs can use `VehicleManager` as follows:

```
VehicleManager manager = new VehicleManager();

Vehicle saloon1 = manager.createSaloon();
Vehicle saloon2 = manager.createSaloon();
Vehicle pickup1 = manager.createPickup();
```

A drawback of `VehicleManager` as coded is that it always instantiates at least one vehicle of each type as part of the construction process. If not all types of vehicles will be needed, a more efficient technique would be to lazy-load by only instantiating the first time each is needed. This is illustrated in the modified version of the class (which we will call `VehicleManagerLazy`) below:

```
public class VehicleManagerLazy {

    private Vehicle saloon, coupe, sport, boxVan, pickup;

    public VehicleManagerLazy() {
    }

    public Vehicle createSaloon() {
        if (saloon == null) {
            saloon = new Saloon(new StandardEngine(1300));
            return saloon;
        } else {
            return (Vehicle) saloon.clone();
        }
    }

    public Vehicle createCoupe() {
        if (coupe == null) {
            coupe = new Coupe(new StandardEngine(1300));
            return coupe;
        } else {
            return (Vehicle) coupe.clone();
        }
    }

    public Vehicle createSport() {
```

```
        if (sport == null) {
            sport = new Sport(new StandardEngine(1300));
            return sport;
        } else {
            return (Vehicle) sport.clone();
        }
    }

    public Vehicle createBoxVan() {
        if (boxVan == null) {
            boxVan = new BoxVan(new StandardEngine(1300));
            return boxVan;
        } else {
            return (Vehicle) boxVan.clone();
        }
    }

    public Vehicle createPickup() {
        if (pickup == null) {
            pickup = new Pickup(new StandardEngine(1300));
            return pickup;
        } else {
            return (Vehicle) pickup.clone();
        }
    }

}
```

Before a clone is returned, a check is made to ensure that the 'prototype' object exists, and it will be instantiated if necessary. From then on it just clones the previously instantiated object. Client programs can use VehicleManagerLazy in the same way as before:

```
VehicleManagerLazy manager = new VehicleManagerLazy();

Vehicle saloon1 = manager.createSaloon();
Vehicle saloon2 = manager.createSaloon();
Vehicle pickup1 = manager.createPickup();
```

6. Singleton

Type	Creational
Purpose	Ensure a class allows only one object to be created, providing a single point of access to it.

The Foobar Motor Company, in common with all vehicle manufacturers, needs to stamp a unique serial number on all vehicles they produce[1]. They want to model this requirement ensuring that there is just one easy place where the next available serial number can be obtained. If we were to have more than one object that generates the next number there is a risk that we could end up with separate numbering sequences, so we need to prevent this.

The *Singleton* pattern provides a way of ensuring that only one instance of a particular class can ever be created. So how can we stop other objects from just invoking new multiple times? There are several ways of accomplishing this, and the "traditional" approach that you may often encounter is to make your constructor private but provide a public static getter method that returns a static instance of the *Singleton* class. This is how it could look:

```
public class SerialNumberGeneratorTraditional {

    // static members
    private static SerialNumberGeneratorTraditional instance;

    public synchronized static
            SerialNumberGeneratorTraditional getInstance() {
        if (instance == null) {
            instance = new SerialNumberGeneratorTraditional();
        }
        return instance;
    }

    // instance variables
    private int count;
```

---

[1] In the UK this is known as the Vehicle Identification Number (VIN).

```
    // private constructor
    private SerialNumberGeneratorTraditional() {}

    // instance methods
    public synchronized int getNextSerial() {
        return ++count;
    }
}
```

Note that the getInstance() method will only instantiate the object once and so the same instance will always be returned. The constructor is private to prevent client programs from calling new, thus enforcing the fact that only one object can ever be created, since they can only go through the getInstance() method. The getInstance() and getNextSerial() methods are synchronized in case they are called by separate threads. The singleton could be used thus:

```
System.out.println("Using traditional singleton");
SerialNumberGeneratorTraditional generator =
            SerialNumberGeneratorTraditional.getInstance();
System.out.println("next serial: " + generator.getNextSerial());
System.out.println("next serial: " + generator.getNextSerial());
System.out.println("next serial: " + generator.getNextSerial());
```

An arguably better way of coding singletons has existed since Java 1.5 by utilising the enum type. The above class would then be:

```
public enum SerialNumberGenerator {

    INSTANCE;

    private int count;

    public synchronized int getNextSerial() {
        return ++count;
    }

}
```

The constant name INSTANCE represents the singleton. As in the traditional approach there is an instance variable count and synchronized method getNextSerial(), but now there is no need to define any static members or worry about a constructor.

Using the enum singleton is as simple as this:

```
System.out.println("Using enum singleton");
System.out.println("next vehicle: " +
                SerialNumberGenerator.INSTANCE.getNextSerial());
System.out.println("next vehicle: " +
                SerialNumberGenerator.INSTANCE.getNextSerial());
System.out.println("next engine: " +
                SerialNumberGenerator.INSTANCE.getNextSerial());
```

Sometimes you may want a specific number of different singletons that perform the same actions (a so-called *Multiton*, a contraction of "multiple singleton"). This is not that straightforward using the traditional approach, but when using the enum technique it is as easy as defining separate constants. For example, suppose you now need separate serial numbers for vehicles and engines where each increment independently of each other:

```
public enum SerialNumberGenerator {

    VEHICLE, ENGINE;

    private int count;

    public synchronized int getNextSerial() {
        return ++count;
    }

}
```

The constant INSTANCE has been renamed as VEHICLE and a second constant ENGINE has been defined. You can access these as follows:

```
System.out.println("Using enum singleton");
System.out.println("next vehicle: " +
                SerialNumberGenerator.VEHICLE.getNextSerial());
System.out.println("next vehicle: " +
                SerialNumberGenerator.VEHICLE.getNextSerial());
System.out.println("next engine: " +
                SerialNumberGenerator.ENGINE.getNextSerial());
System.out.println("next vehicle: " +
                SerialNumberGenerator.VEHICLE.getNextSerial());
System.out.println("next engine: " +
                SerialNumberGenerator.ENGINE.getNextSerial());
```

The output of which should be:

```
Next vehicle: 1
Next vehicle: 2
Next engine: 1
Next vehicle: 3
Next engine: 2
```

Part III. Structural Patterns

This part describes the seven structural patterns, that is, those that help manage how classes are organised and interrelate.

- *Adapter:* Convert the interface of a class into the interface clients expect, letting classes work together that couldn't otherwise because of incompatible types;

- *Bridge:* Decouple an abstraction from its implementation so that each may vary independently;

- *Composite:* Compose objects into tree structures to represent part-whole hierarchies, letting client objects treat individual objects and compositions uniformly;

- *Decorator:* Attach additional responsibilities to an object dynamically;

- *Façade:* Provide a uniform interface to a set of interfaces in a subsystem, by defining a higher-level interface that makes the subsystem easier to use;

- *Flyweight:* Use sharing to support large numbers of fine-grained objects efficiently;

- *Proxy:* Provide a surrogate or place-holder for another object to control access to it.

7.   Adapter

Type	Structural
Purpose	Convert the interface of a class into another interface clients expect. *Adapter* lets classes work together that couldn't otherwise because of incompatible interfaces.

You will recall from the introduction that the Foobar Motor Company makes the engines for their vehicles. Here is a reminder of the Engine hierarchy:

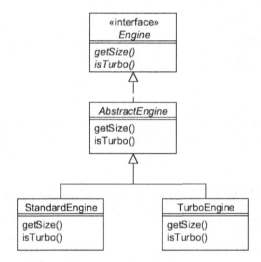

Figure 7.1 : Engine class hierarchy

And here is a reminder of the code of the abstract AbstractEngine class:

```
public abstract class AbstractEngine implements Engine {

    private int size;
    private boolean turbo;

    public AbstractEngine(int size, boolean turbo) {
        this.size = size;
        this.turbo = turbo;
```

```
        }

    public int getSize() {
        return size;
    }

    public boolean isTurbo() {
        return turbo;
    }

    public String toString() {
        return getClass().getSimpleName() +
                " (" + size + ")");
    }

}
```

Let's say our client program takes engines stored in a collection and loops through them one at a time displaying the engine size and type:

```
List<Engine> engines = new ArrayList<Engine>();

engines.add(new StandardEngine(1300));
engines.add(new StandardEngine(1600));
engines.add(new TurboEngine(2000));

for (Engine engine : engines) {
    System.out.println(engine);
}
```

Running the above code would result in the following display:

```
StandardEngine (1300)
StandardEngine (1600)
TurboEngine (2000)
```

For this chapter we will assume that in addition to the two concrete subclasses (StandardEngine and TurboEngine) Foobar have decided to use a further engine class named SuperGreenEngine which is made by a different manufacturer.

Because the SuperGreenEngine class is provided by a third-party it does not implement our Engine interface. Furthermore, Foobar do not have access to the Java source code and can therefore not modify it, but the following class details are known from the documentation:

- The class extends `Object`;

- The constructor takes one argument for the engine size;

- There is a `getEngineSize()` method that returns the engine size as an int;

- These types of engines are never turbocharged;

- The `toString()` method returns a `String` in the format: SUPER ENGINE nnnn (where nnnn is the engine size).

We can therefore see that `SuperGreenEngine` uses a different method name to access the engine size and there is no method related to whether it is turbocharged, and that it is not within the `Engine` hierarchy. As it stands it would not be possible to add instances of `SuperGreenEngine` to the reporting collection and even if you could the method names are different.

The *Adapter* pattern provides an approach to resolve this through the definition of a new class that 'adapts' the class we want to use into the format existing classes require. For our purposes, therefore, we shall create a `SuperGreenEngineAdapter` class:

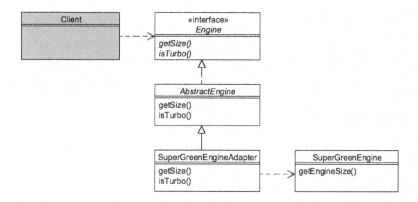

Figure 7.2 : Adapter class hierarchy

The code for the adapter is as follows:

```java
public class SuperGreenEngineAdapter extends AbstractEngine {

    public SuperGreenEngineAdapter(SuperGreenEngine greenEngine) {
        super(greenEngine.getEngineSize(), false);
    }

}
```

Note the following from the above Java code:

*   We extend the class we are adapting **to**.

*   We accept a reference in the constructor to the class we are adapting **from**.

*   The constructor obtains the necessary state from the referenced object and passes it to the superclass constructor.

Now we are in a position to include `SuperGreenEngine` objects in our reporting collection (additional code indicated in bold):

```java
List<Engine> engines = new ArrayList<Engine>();
engines.add(new StandardEngine(1300));
engines.add(new StandardEngine(1600));
engines.add(new TurboEngine(2000));

// "Adapt" the new engine type...
SuperGreenEngine greenEngine = new SuperGreenEngine(1200);
engines.add(new SuperGreenEngineAdapter(greenEngine));

// Unchanged from before...
for (Engine engine : engines) {
    System.out.println(engine);
}
```

The output should now be:

```
StandardEngine (1300)
StandardEngine (1600)
TurboEngine (2000)
SuperGreenEngine (1200)
```

Note how the output made use of the `toString()` method as inherited from `AbstractEngine` rather than that of `SuperGreenEngine`.

Variations for implementing adapters

We were somewhat fortunate in that the design of the `Engine` and `SuperGreenEngine` classes made it easy for the adapter class to do the work inside its constructor. Often however, we need to take a few additional steps inside the code of the adapter class, so here is a general formula to apply:

1. Extend the class you are adapting to (or implement it, if it's an interface);

2. Specify the class you are adapting from in the constructor and store a reference to it in an instance variable;

3. For each method in the class you are extending (or interface you are implementing), override it to delegate to the corresponding method of the class you are adapting from.

Here is a generic example adapter class:

```
public class ObjectAdapter extends ClassAdaptingTo {

    private ClassAdaptingFrom fromObject;

    public ObjectAdapter(ClassAdaptingFrom fromObject) {
        this.fromObject = fromObject;
    }

    // Overridden method
    public void methodInToClass() {
        fromObject.methodInFromClass();
    }

}
```

8. Bridge

Type	Structural
Purpose	Decouple an abstraction from its implementation so that each may vary independently.

The Foobar Motor Company manufactures engines for its vehicles. Here is a reminder of the Engine class hierarchy:

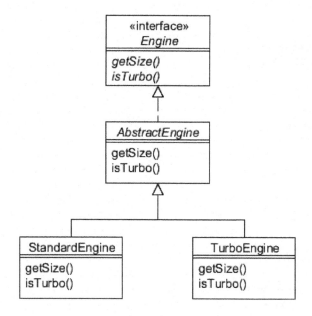

Figure 8.1 : Engine class hierarchy

The implementation of the Engine class as detailed in the introduction, merely stores the engine size (e.g. 1600cc) and whether it is turbocharged. For the purposes of this chapter this class will be enhanced to enable the engine to be started and stopped and for the power to the engine to be increased or decreased.

The modified version of the `Engine` interface and `AbstractEngine` class is listed below with the changes marked in bold:

```
public interface Engine {

    public int getSize();
    public boolean isTurbo();

    public void start();
    public void stop();
    public void increasePower();
    public void decreasePower();

}
```

```
public abstract class AbstractEngine implements Engine {

    private int size;
    private boolean turbo;
    private boolean running;
    private int power;

    public AbstractEngine(int size, boolean turbo) {
        this.size = size;
        this.turbo = turbo;
        running = false;
        power = 0;
    }

    public int getSize() {
        return size;
    }

    public boolean isTurbo() {
        return turbo;
    }

    public void start() {
        running = true;
        System.out.println("Engine started");
    }

    public void stop() {
        running = false;
        power = 0;
        System.out.println("Engine stopped");
    }

    public void increasePower() {
        if (running && (power < 10)) {
            power++;
            System.out.println("Engine power increased to " + power);
        }
    }
```

```
public void decreasePower() {
    if (running && (power > 0)) {
        power--;
        System.out.println("Engine power decreased to " + power);
    }
}

public String toString() {
    return getClass().getSimpleName() +
            " (" + size ")");
}

}
```

Within a vehicle, the driver controls the functions of the engine indirectly by means of various hand and foot controls, such as the ignition switch, accelerator pedal and brake pedal. To retain flexibility, it is important to design the connection between the engine and the controls so that each can vary independently of the other. In other words:

- *A new engine can be designed and plugged into a vehicle without needing any driver controls to be changed; and*

- *New driver controls (for example, to assist disabled drivers) can be designed and plugged into a vehicle without needing the engines to change.*

The *Bridge* pattern addresses this requirement by separating the 'abstraction' from the 'implementation' into two separate but connected hierarchies such that each can vary independently of the other. In our example, the 'abstraction' is the driver controls and the 'implementation' is the engine.

The following diagram shows this relationship:

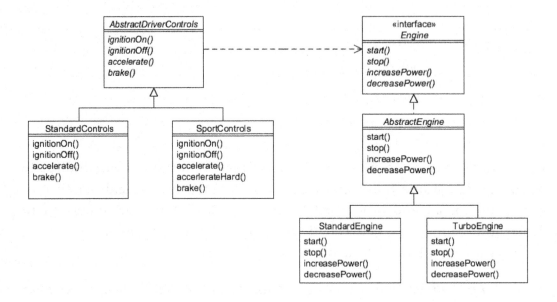

Figure 8.2 : Bridge pattern

As the above figure shows, there is an abstract `AbstractDriverControls` class with two concrete subclasses; `StandardControls` and `SportControls`:

The `AbstractDriverControls` class requires an `Engine` object passed to its constructor and then delegates to the engine for each of its methods:

```
public abstract class AbstractDriverControls {

    private Engine engine;

    public AbstractDriverControls(Engine engine) {
        this.engine = engine;
    }

    public void ignitionOn() {
        engine.start();
    }
```

```
public void ignitionOff() {
    engine.stop();
}

public void accelerate() {
    engine.increasePower();
}

public void brake() {
    engine.decreasePower();
}
```

}

Subclasses of `AbstractDriverControls` can either use the superclass methods as-is or define additional functionality:

The `StandardControls` class uses `AbstractDriverControls` as-is:

```
public class StandardControls extends AbstractDriverControls {

    public StandardControls(Engine engine) {
        super(engine);
    }

    // No extra features

}
```

Whereas the `SportControls` class defines an additional method:

```
public class SportControls extends AbstractDriverControls {

    public SportControls(Engine engine) {
        super(eengine);
    }

    public void accelerateHard() {
        accelerate();
        accelerate();
    }

}
```

The important point to note from the above is that the additional method is coded in terms of the superclass 'abstraction' and *not* the 'implementation' (engine). So in the above example the `accelerateHard()` method invokes the `accelerate()` method as defined in `AbstractDriverControls`. It is this approach that allows the abstraction and the implementation to vary independently if needed.

Thus we could incorporate a brand-new type of engine without modifying the driver controls classes, provided the engine adheres to the `Engine` contract. Conversely we could develop a new set of driver controls (such as enabling voice activation) without having to modify anything in the `Engine` hierarchy.

Client programs can use the bridge as follows:

```
Engine engine = new StandardEngine(1300);
StandardControls controls1 = new StandardControls(engine);
controls1.ignitionOn();
controls1.accelerate();
controls1.brake();
controls1.ignitionOff();

// Now use sport controls
SportControls controls2 = new SportControls(engine);
controls2.ignitionOn();
controls2.accelerate();
controls2.accelerateHard();
controls2.brake();
controls2.ignitionOff();
```

9.   Composite

Type	Structural
Purpose	Compose objects into tree structures to represent part-whole hierarchies. *Composite* lets clients treat individual objects and compositions of objects uniformly.

In the Foobar Motor Company workshop they build various items from component parts such as nuts, bolts, panels, etc. Each individual component item has an associated description and unit cost, and when items are assembled into larger items the cost is therefore the sum of its component parts[1].

The *Composite* pattern enables us to treat both individual parts and assemblies of parts as if they are the same, thus enabling them to be processed in a consistent manner, simplifying code. The class hierarchy looks like this:

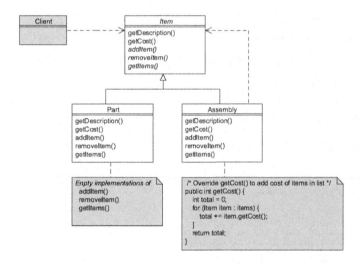

Figure 9.1 : Composite pattern

---

[1] We will ignore the cost of assembly, such as labour costs.

The abstract `Item` class defines all possible methods for both parts and assemblies of parts:

```
public abstract class Item {

    private String description;
    private int cost;

    public Item(String description, int cost) {
        this.description = description;
        this.cost = cost;
    }

    public String getDescription() {
        return description;
    }

    public int getCost() {
        return cost;
    }

    public abstract void addItem(Item item);
    public abstract void removeItem(Item item);
    public abstract Item[] getItems();

    public String toString() {
        return description + " (cost " + getCost() + ")";
    }

}
```

The above class provides default implementations for `getDescription()` and `getCost()`, and defines the abstract methods `addItem()`, `removeItem()` and `getItems()`.

Individual parts are modelled using the `Part` subclass:

```
public class Part extends Item {

    public Part(String description, int cost) {
        super(description, cost);
    }

    // Empty implementation for unit parts...
    public void addItem(Item item) {}
    public void removeItem(Item item) {}
    public Item[] getItems() {return new Item[0];}
}
```

As you can see, the methods related to managing assemblies of items have empty implementations since a 'part' is the smallest unit possible, and therefore unable to have sub-parts, unlike 'assemblies'.

Assemblies of parts are modelled using the `Assembly` subclass:

```java
public class Assembly extends Item {

    private List<Item> items;

    public Assembly(String description) {
        super(description, 0);
        items = new ArrayList<Item>();
    }

    public void addItem(Item item) {
        items.add(item);
    }

    public void removeItem(Item item) {
        items.remove(item);
    }

    public Item[] getItems() {
        return items.toArray(new Item[items.size()]);
    }

    // Also have to override getCost() to add cost of items in list
    public int getCost() {
        int total = 0;
        for (Item item : items) {
            total += item.getCost();
        }
        return total;
    }
}
```

For assemblies, we have implemented the abstract methods to add other `Item` objects into an internal `List` collection. We have also overridden the `getCost()` method to loop through the collection to sum the cost of all contained items within this assembly.[1]

All types of `Item` objects can now be used in a uniform manner:

```java
Item nut = new Part("Nut", 5);
Item bolt = new Part("Bolt", 9);
```

---

[1]We set the cost to zero when constructing `Assembly` object, since initially it has no component parts until they are added.

```
Item panel = new Part("Panel", 35);

Item gizmo = new Assembly("Gizmo");
gizmo.addItem(panel);
gizmo.addItem(nut);
gizmo.addItem(bolt);

Item widget = new Assembly("Widget");
widget.addItem(gizmo);
widget.addItem(nut);
```

In the above extract, nuts, bolts and panels are defined as individual parts, a "Gizmo" is assembled from one nut, one bolt and one panel, and a "Widget" is assembled from one "Gizmo" and another nut.

Displaying the objects would result in this:

```
Nut (cost 5)
Bolt (cost 9)
Panel (cost 35)
Gizmo (cost 49)
Widget (cost 54)
```

The assemblies have computed the total cost without the client program needing to know how.

10. Decorator

Type	Structural
Purpose	Attach additional responsibilities to an object dynamically. Decorators provide a flexible alternative to subclassing for extending functionality.

You will recall the Foobar Motor Company Vehicle class hierarchy:

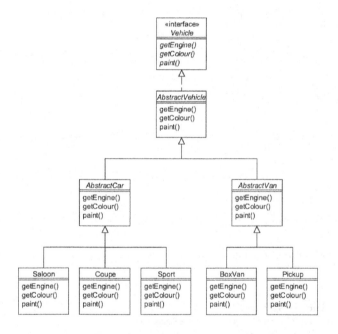

Figure 10.1 : Vehicle class hierarchy

For the purposes of this chapter, we shall add one additional method called getPrice() to the Vehicle interface. We will also modify the toString() method in AbstractVehicle to include the price. The modified interface and class is shown below with the changes marked in bold:

```
public interface Vehicle {
```

```
        public enum Colour {UNPAINTED, BLUE, BLACK, GREEN,
                            RED, SILVER, WHITE, YELLOW};

        public Engine getEngine();
        public void paint(Vehicle.Colour colour);
        public Vehicle.Colour getColour();
        public int getPrice();


    }



public abstract class AbstractVehicle implements Vehicle {

    private Engine engine;
    private Vehicle.Colour colour;


    public AbstractVehicle(Engine engine) {
        this(engine, Vehicle.Colour.UNPAINTED);
    }

    public AbstractVehicle(Engine engine, Vehicle.Colour colour) {
        this.engine = engine;
        this.colour = colour;
    }

    public Engine getEngine() {
        return engine;
    }

    public Vehicle.Colour getColour() {
        return colour;
    }

    public void paint(Vehicle.Colour colour) {
        colour = colour;
    }

    public String toString() {
        return getClass().getSimpleName() +
                " (" + engine + ", " + colour +
                ", price " + getPrice() + ")";
    }


}
```

Each of the concrete subclasses implements the getPrice() method as appropriate. For example, the Saloon class now looks like this (changes in bold):

```
public class Saloon extends AbstractCar {
```

```
public Saloon(Engine engine) {
    this(engine, Vehicle.Colour.UNPAINTED)
}

public Saloon(Engine engine, Vehicle.Colour colour) {
    super(engine, colour);
}

public int getPrice() {
    return 6000;
}

}
```

The other subclasses are similarly defined, and the getPrice() method returns:

- 6,000 for Saloon objects;

- 7,000 for Coupe objects;

- 8,000 for Sport objects;

- 9,000 for Pickup objects;

- 10,000 for BoxVan objects.

When a customer buys a vehicle they have the choice of adding any number of optional extras. They can choose from an air-conditioning system, alloy wheels, leather seats, metallic paint, or a satellite-navigation unit. They can choose none at all, or any combination up to all five.

The *Decorator* pattern is designed to facilitate the addition of state and/or behaviour without having to modify the inheritance hierarchy of the classes being added to. This is accomplished by defining a new hierarchy which itself extends the root of the main tree.

This is shown diagrammatically below:

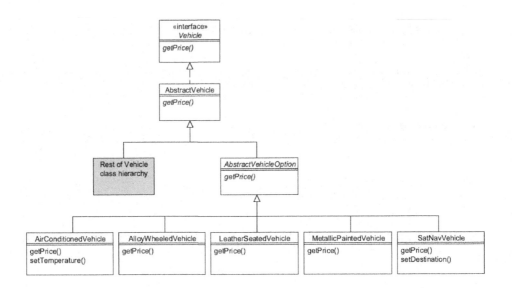

Figure 10.2 : Decorator pattern hierarchy

From the diagram you can see that a new abstract class has been defined called `AbstractVehicleOption` that inherits from `AbstractVehicle`. `AbstractVehicleOption` has five concrete subclasses; one for each option that can be selected.

The `AbstractVehicleOption` class looks like this:

```
public abstract class AbstractVehicleOption extends AbstractVehicle {

    protected Vehicle decoratedVehicle;

    public AbstractVehicleOption(Vehicle vehicle) {
        super(vehicle.getEngine());
        decoratedVehicle = vehicle;
    }

}
```

`AbstractVehicleOption` is the abstract "decorator" class and it requires a reference to the `Vehicle` class which is to be decorated.

Each of the option subclasses is straightforward. They all override the getPrice() method to add the price of the option to the price of the object that is being decorated. In the case of the AirConditionedVehicle and SatNavVehicle classes, we have also defined an extra method:

```
public class AirConditionedVehicle extends AbstractVehicleOption {

    public AirConditioning(Vehicle vehicle) {
        super(vehicle);
    }

    public int getPrice() {
        return decoratedVehicle.getPrice() + 600;
    }

    public void setTemperature(int value) {
        // code to set the temperature...
    }

}



public class AlloyWheeledVehicle extends AbstractVehicleOption {

    public AlloyWheels(Vehicle vehicle) {
        super(vehicle);
    }

    public int getPrice() {
        return decoratedVehicle.getPrice() + 250;
    }

}



public class LeatherSeatedVehicle extends AbstractVehicleOption {

    public LeatherSeats(Vehicle vehicle) {
        super(vehicle);
    }

    public int getPrice() {
        return decoratedVehicle.getPrice() + 1200;
    }

}



public class MetallicPaintedVehicle extends AbstractVehicleOption {

    public MetallicPaint(Vehicle vehicle) {
        super(vehicle);
```

```
        }

    public int getPrice() {
        return decoratedVehicle.getPrice() + 750;
    }

}


public class SatNavVehicle extends AbstractVehicleOption {

    public SatNav(Vehicle vehicle) {
        super(vehicle);
    }

    public int getPrice() {
        return decoratedVehicle.getPrice() + 1500;
    }

    public void setDestination(String target) {
        // code to set the destination...
    }

}
```

To use the 'decorators' we initially instantiate the car or van we require and then "wrap" them inside the required decorator or decorators.

Here is an example:

```
// Create a blue saloon car...
Vehicle myCar = new Saloon(new StandardEngine(1300));
myCar.paint(Vehicle.Colour.BLUE);

// Add air-conditioning to the car...
myCar = new AirConditionedVehicle(myCar);

// Now add alloy wheels...
myCar = new AlloyWheeledVehicle(myCar);

// Now add leather seats...
myCar = new LeatherSeatedVehicle(myCar);

// Now add metallic paint...
myCar = new MetallicPaintedVehicle(myCar);

// Now add satellite-navigation...
myCar = new SatNavVehicle(myCar);
```

If you invoke `System.out.prinln()` on the `myCar` object at each stage you should see this output:

```
Saloon (StandardEngine (1300), BLUE, price 6000)
AirConditionedVehicle (StandardEngine (1300), BLUE, price 6600)
AlloyWheeledVehicle (StandardEngine (1300), BLUE, price 6850)
LeatherSeatedVehicle (StandardEngine (1300), BLUE, price 8050)
MetallicPaintedVehicle (StandardEngine (1300), BLUE, price 8800)
SatNavVehicle (StandardEngine (1300), BLUE, price 10300)
```

The price shown at each stage is the total of the vehicle plus the selected options as each is "added".

The *Decorator* pattern is a good example of preferring object composition over inheritance. Had we attempted to use inheritance for the various vehicle options we would have needed to create many different combinations of subclasses to model each combination of selectable options.

Decorator classes are sometimes called "wrapper" classes, since they serve to "wrap" an object inside another object, usually to add or modify its functionality.

11. Facade

Type	Structural
Purpose	Provide a unified interface to a set of interfaces in a subsystem. *Facade* defines a higher-level interface that makes the subsystem easier to use.

Sometimes you need to perform a series of steps to undertake a particular task, often involving multiple objects. The *Facade* pattern involves the creation of a separate object that simplifies the execution of such steps.

As an example, when the Foobar Motor Company are preparing their vehicles for sale there are a number of steps they have to undertake that utilise various objects. In this chapter we shall assume that the Vehicle interface defines the following additional methods beyond those defined in the introduction.

```
// Extra methods defined in Vehicle...

public void cleanInterior();
public void cleanExteriorBody();
public void polishWindows();
public void takeForTestDrive();
```

The above methods are implemented in AbstractVehicle as follows:

```
public void cleanInterior() {
    System.out.println("Cleaning interior");
}

public void cleanExteriorBody() {
    System.out.println("Cleaning exterior");
}

public void polishWindows() {
    System.out.println("polishing windows");
}

public void takeForTestDrive() {
    System.out.println("taking for test drive");
}
```

We shall introduce two further simple classes called `Registration` and `Documentation`:

```
public class Registration {

    private Vehicle vehicle;

    public Registration(Vehicle vehicle) {
        this.vehicle = vehicle;
    }

    public void allocateLicensePlate() {
        // Code omitted...
        System.out.println("License plate allocated");
    }

    public void allocateVehicleNumber() {
        // Code omitted...
        System.out.println("Vehicle number allocated");
    }

}


public class Documentation {

    public static void printBrochure(Vehicle vehicle) {
        // code omitted...
        System.out.println("Brochure printed");
    }

}
```

To implement the pattern we will create a `VehicleFacade` class that defines a method to prepare the specified vehicle by using the above classes on our behalf:

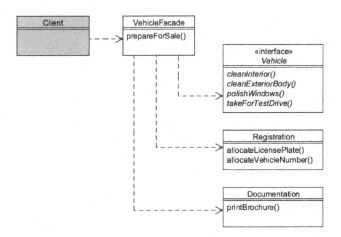

Figure 11.1 : Facade pattern

```
public class VehicleFacade {

    public void prepareForSale(Vehicle vehicle) {
        Registration reg = new Registration(vehicle);
        reg.allocateVehicleNumber();
        reg.allocateLicensePlate();

        Documentation.printBrochure(vehicle);

        vehicle.cleanInterior();
        vehicle.cleanExteriorBody();
        vehicle.polishWindows();
        vehicle.takeForTestDrive();
    }

}
```

Client programs then only need invoke the `prepareForSale()` method on a `VehicleFacade` instance, and therefore need no knowledge of what needs to be done and what other objects are needed. And if something different is needed in a special circumstance, then the individual methods are still available for calling as required.

12. Flyweight

Type	Structural
Purpose	Use sharing to support large numbers of fine-grained objects efficiently.

Some programs need to create a large number of objects of one particular type, and if those objects happen to have a large amount of state then instantiating lots of them can quickly use up memory. When considering object state, we often note that at least some of it could potentially be shared among a group of objects.

For the Foobar Motor Company, the Engine hierarchy is a case in point:

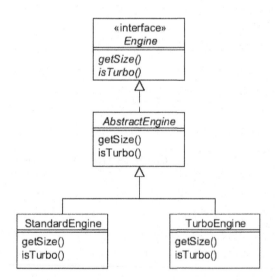

Figure 12.1 : Engine class hierarchy

Our simple implementation of Engine only defines two methods; getSize() and isTurbo(). Let's suppose we instantiate two engines as follows:

```
Engine engine1 = new StandardEngine(1300);
Engine engine2 = new StandardEngine(1300);
```

The above would create two separate objects in memory, even though their state is identical. This can be thought of as its *intrinsic state*; i.e. all 1300cc standard engines will be storing *1300* for the engine size and `false` for whether it is turbocharged. Creating hundreds or thousands of these would be wasteful of memory, especially since a more realistic `Engine` class would require many more variables whose values would also be shared.

For the purposes of this chapter another method will be added to the `Engine` interface, called `diagnose()`. This new method will take a `DiagnosticTool` object as its argument, and this argument can be thought of as its *extrinsic state*, since its value is not actually stored in the `Engine` object – it is used purely so that the engine can use it to run a diagnostic check.

The `DiagnosticTool` interface looks like this:

```java
public interface DiagnosticTool {

    public void runDiagnosis(Object obj);

}
```

The `EngineDiagnosticTool` implements the above for running diagnostics on an engine:

```java
public class EngineDiagnosticTool implements DiagnosticTool {

    public void runDiagnosis(Object obj) {
        System.out.println("Starting engine diagnostic tool for " +
                                                               obj);
        try {
            Thread.sleep(5000);
            System.out.println("Engine diagnosis complete");
        } catch (InterruptedException ex) {
            System.out.println("Engine diagnosis interrupted");
        }
    }

}
```

To simulate a long-running process the method pauses for five seconds.

With the above in place we can now add a suitable method to the Engine interface:

```
public interface Engine {

     // Methods having intrinsic (i.e. shared) state
     public int getSize();
     public boolean isTurbo();

     // Methods having extrinsic (i.e. unshared) state
     public void diagnose(DiagnosticTool tool);

}
```

The implementation of this new method in AbstractEngine simply issues a call-back to the DiagnosticTool:

```
public void diagnose(DiagnosticTool tool) {
     tool.runDiagnosis(this);
}
```

The *Flyweight* pattern allows you to reference a multitude of objects of the same type and having the same state, but only by instantiating the minimum number of actual objects needed. This is typically done by allocating a 'pool' of objects which can be shared, and this is determined by a 'flyweight factory' class. Client programs get access to engines only through the factory:

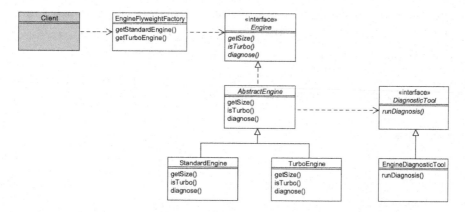

Figure 12.2 : Flyweight pattern

The `EngineFlyweightFactory` class looks like this:

```
public class EngineFlyweightFactory {

    private Map<Integer, Engine> standardEnginePool;
    private Map<Integer, Engine> turboEnginePool;

    public EngineFlyweightFactory() {
        standardEnginePool = new HashMap<Integer, Engine>();
        turboEnginePool = new HashMap<Integer, Engine>();
    }

    public Engine getStandardEngine(int size) {
        Engine e = standardEnginePool.get(size);
        if (e == null) {
            e = new StandardEngine(size);
            standardEnginePool.put(size, e);
        }
        return e;
    }

    public Engine getTurboEngine(int size) {
        Engine e = turboEnginePool.get(size);
        if (e == null) {
            e = new TurboEngine(size);
            turboEnginePool.put(size, e);
        }
        return e;
    }

}
```

This class utilises two maps (one for standard engines and the other for turbo engines). Each time an engine of a particular type and size is requested, if a similar one has already been created it is returned rather than instantiating a new one.

Client programs use the factory like this:

```
// Create the flyweight factory...
EngineFlyweightFactory factory = new EngineFlyweightFactory();

// Create the diagnostic tool
DiagnosticTool tool = new EngineDiagnosticTool();

// Get the flyweights and run diagnostics on them
Engine standard1 = factory.getStandardEngine(1300);
standard1.diagnose(tool);
```

```
Engine standard2 = factory.getStandardEngine(1300);
standard2.diagnose(tool);

Engine standard3 = factory.getStandardEngine(1300);
standard3.diagnose(tool);

Engine standard4 = factory.getStandardEngine(1600);
standard4.diagnose(tool);

Engine standard5 = factory.getStandardEngine(1600);
standard5.diagnose(tool);

// Show that objects are shared
System.out.println(standard1.hashCode());
System.out.println(standard2.hashCode());
System.out.println(standard3.hashCode());
System.out.println(standard4.hashCode());
System.out.println(standard5.hashCode());
```

In the above, the variables standard1, standard2 and standard3 all reference the same Engine object (since they all 1300cc standard engines). Likewise, standard4 references the same object as standard5. Of course, whether it is worth running the diagnostics multiple times on the same objects is arguable depending upon the circumstances!

If the arguments passed to the extrinsic method (DiagnosticTool in our example) need to be stored, this should be done in the client program.

13. Proxy

Type	Structural
Purpose	Provide a surrogate or place-holder for another object to control access to it.

Some methods can be time-consuming, such as those that load complex graphical components or need network connections. In these instances, the *Proxy* pattern provides a 'stand-in' object until such time that the time-consuming resource is complete, allowing the rest of your application to load.

In the chapter discussing the *Flyweight* pattern, the `Engine` hierarchy was enhanced to define the additional method `diagnose()`. As you saw, the implementation of `runDiagnosis()` in `EngineDiagnosticTool` is slow (we made it sleep for five seconds to simulate this), so we might consider making this run is a separate thread.

Here is a reminder of the `Engine` hierarchy with the additional method:

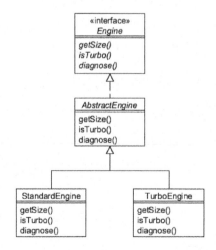

Figure 13.1 : Engine class hierarchy

The *Proxy* pattern involves creating a class that implements the same interface that we are standing-in for, in our case `Engine`. The proxy then forwards requests to the "real" object which it stores internally. Clients just access the proxy:

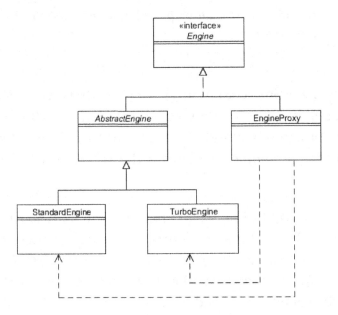

Figure 13.2 : Proxy pattern

Here is the code for the `EngineProxy` class:

```java
public class EngineProxy implements Engine {

    private Engine engine;

    public EngineProxy(int size, boolean turbo) {
        if (turbo) {
            engine = new TurboEngine(size);
        } else {
            engine = new StandardEngine(size);
        }
    }

    public int getSize() {
        return engine.getSize();
    }

    public boolean isTurbo() {
```

```
        return engine.isTurbo();
    }

    // This method is time-consuming...
    public void diagnose(final DiagnosticTool tool) {
        // Run the method as a separate thread
        Thread t = new Thread(new Runnable() {
            public void run() {
                System.out.println("(Running tool as thread)");
                engine.diagnose(tool);
            }
        });
        t.start();
        System.out.println("EngineProxy diagnose() method finished");
    }

}
```

The constructor creates either a `StandardEngine` or `TurboEngine` object and stores a reference to it as an instance variable. Calls to `getSize()` and `isTurbo()` simply forward to the referenced engine object. Calls to `diagnose()` will invoke a separate thread to run the actual diagnosis. This can be useful if you cannot modify the original source for some reason.

This leaves the question of how you can 'force' client programs to use the proxy class instead of the normal class. One approach would be to make the constructors of `StandardEngine` and `TurboEngine` package-private (i.e. using no access modifier); then provided `EngineProxy` is in the same package it will be able to instantiate them but outside objects won't. It is also common to have a 'factory' class to make instantiation simpler, e.g. by providing a `createStandardEngine()` method.

Part IV. Behavioural Patterns

This part describes the eleven behavioural patterns, that is, those that help manage what the classes actually do.

- *Chain of Responsibility*: Avoid coupling the sender of a request to its receiver by giving more than one object the chance to handle the request;

- *Command*: Encapsulate a request as an object, thereby letting you parameterise clients with different requests;

- *Interpreter*: Define the representation of a language's grammar;

- *Iterator*: Provide a way to access the elements of an aggregate object sequentially without exposing its underlying representation;

- *Mediator*: Define an object that encapsulates how a set of objects interact;

- *Memento*: Capture and externalise an object's state so that it can be restored to that state later;

- *Observer*: Define a one-to-many dependency between objects so that when one object changes its state, all of its dependents are notified and updated automatically;

- *State*: Allow an object to alter its behaviour when its internal state changes, as if it were a different class;

- *Strategy*: Allow clients to change the algorithm that an object uses to perform a function;

- *Template Method*: Define the skeleton of an algorithm in a method, deferring some steps to subclasses;

- *Visitor.* Simulate the addition of a method to a class without needing to actually change the class.

14. Chain of Responsibility

Type	Behavioural
Purpose	Avoid coupling the sender of a request to its receiver by giving more than one object a chance to handle the request. Chain the receiving objects and pass the request along the chain until an object handles it.

The Foobar Motor Company receives many emails each day, including servicing requests, sales enquiries, complaints, and of course the inevitable spam. Rather than employ someone specifically to sort through each email to determine which department it should be forwarded to, our task is to try and automate this by analysing the text in each email and making a "best guess".

In our simplified example, we will search the text of the email for a number of keywords and depending upon what we find will process accordingly. Here are the words we will search for and how they should be handled:

Keywords	Forward to
"viagra", "pills", "medicines"	Spam handler
"buy", "purchase"	Sales department
"service", "repair"	Servicing department
"complain", "bad"	Manager
Anything else...	General enquiries

Note that only one object needs to handle the request, so if a particular email contains both "purchase" and "repair" it will be forwarded to the sales department only. The sequence in which to check the keywords is whatever seems most sensible for the application; so here we are trying to filter out spam before it reaches any other department.

Now it would be possible, of course, to just have a series of if...else... statements when checking for the keywords, but that would not be very object-oriented. The *Chain of Responsibility* pattern instead allows us to define separate 'handler' objects that all conform to an EmailHandler interface. This enables us to keep each handler independent and loosely-coupled.

The following diagram shows the pattern:

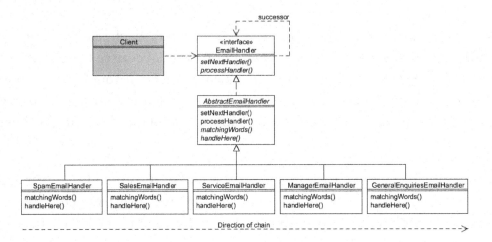

Figure 14.1 : Chain of Responsibility pattern

EmailHandler is the interface at the top of the hierarchy:

```
public interface EmailHandler {

    public void setNextHandler(EmailHandler handler);
    public void processHandler(String email);

}
```

The setNextHandler() method takes another EmailHandler object as its argument which represents the handler to call if the current object is unable to handle the email.

The `processHandler()` method takes the email text as its argument and determines if it is able to handle it (i.e. if it contains one of the keywords we are interested in). If the active object can handle the email it does so, otherwise it just forwards to the next in the chain.

The `AbstractEmailHandler` class implements the `EmailHandler` interface to provide useful default functionality:

```
public abstract class AbstractEmailHandler implements EmailHandler {

    private EmailHandler nextHandler;

    public void setNextHandler(EmailHandler handler) {
        nextHandler = handler;
    }
    public void processHandler(String email) {
        boolean wordFound = false;

        // If no words to match against then this object can handle
        if (matchingWords().length == 0) {
            wordFound = true;

        } else {
            // Look for any of the matching words
            for (String word : matchingWords()) {
                if (email.indexOf(word) >= 0) {
                    wordFound = true;
                    break;
                }
            }
        }

        // Can we handle email in this object?
        if (wordFound) {
            handleHere(email);
        } else {
            // Unable to handle here so forward to next in chain
            nextHandler.processHandler(email);
        }
    }

    protected abstract String[] matchingWords();
    protected abstract void handleHere(String email);

}
```

The method `setNextHandler()` simply stores the argument in an instance variable; the decision making process is made in `processHandler()`. This has been written to utilise two `protected` helper methods that must be implemented by concrete subclasses:

- `matchingWords()` will return an array of `String` objects that this handler is interested in;

- `handleHere()` is only called if this object can actually handle the email and contains whatever code is required.

The concrete subclasses are straightforward:

```java
public class SpamEmailHandler extends AbstractEmailHandler {

    protected String[] matchingWords() {
        return new String[]{"viagra", "pills", "medicines"};
    }

    protected void handleHere(String email) {
        System.out.println("This is a spam email.");
    }

}


public class SalesEmailHandler extends AbstractEmailHandler {

    protected String[] matchingWords() {
        return new String[]{"buy", "purchase"};
    }

    protected void handleHere(String email) {
        System.out.println("Email handled by sales department.");
    }

}


public class ServiceEmailHandler extends AbstractEmailHandler {

    protected String[] matchingWords() {
        return new String[]{"service", "repair"};
    }

    protected void handleHere(String email) {
        System.out.println("Email handled by service department.");
```

```
        }

    }


public class ManagerEmailHandler extends AbstractEmailHandler {

    protected String[] matchingWords() {
        return new String[]{"complain", "bad"};
    }

    protected void handleHere(String email) {
        System.out.println("Email handled by manager.");
    }

}



public class GeneralEnquiriesEmailHandler extends
                                        AbstractEmailHandler {

    protected String[] matchingWords() {
        return new String[0]; // match anything
    }

    protected void handleHere(String email) {
        System.out.println("Email handled by general enquiries.");
    }

}
```

We now need to define the sequence in which the handlers are called. For this example, the following static method has been added to AbstractEmailHandler:

```
public static void handle(String email) {
    // Create the handler objects...
    EmailHandler spam = new SpamEmailHandler();
    EmailHandler sales = new SalesEmailHandler();
    EmailHandler service = new ServiceEmailHandler();
    EmailHandler manager = new ManagerEmailHandler();
    EmailHandler general = new GeneralEnquiriesEmailHandler();

    // Chain them together...
    spam.setNextHandler(sales);
    sales.setNextHandler(service);
    service.setNextHandler(manager);
    manager.setNextHandler(general);

    // Start the ball rolling...
    spam.processHandler(email);
}
```

Putting a message through the handlers is now as simple as this:

```
String email = "I need my car repaired.";
AbstractEmailHandler.handle(email);
```

This should produce the following output:

```
Email handled by service department.
```

15. Command

Type	Behavioural
Purpose	Encapsulate a request as an object, thereby letting you parameterise clients with different requests, queue or log requests, and support undoable operations.

The vehicles made by the Foobar Motor Company each have an installed radio; this is modelled by the following `Radio` class:

```
public class Radio {

    public static final int MIN_VOLUME = 0;
    public static final int MAX_VOLUME = 10;
    public static final int DEFAULT_VOLUME = 5;

    private boolean on;
    private int volume;

    public Radio() {
        on = false;
        volume = DEFAULT_VOLUME;
    }

    public boolean isOn() {
        return on;
    }

    public int getVolume() {
        return volume;
    }

    public void on() {
        on = true;
        System.out.println("Radio now on, volume level " +
                           getVolume());
    }

    public void off() {
        on = false;
        System.out.println("Radio now off");
    }

    public void volumeUp() {
        if (isOn()) {
            if (getVolume() < MAX_VOLUME) {
                volume++;
                System.out.println("Volume turned up to level " +
```

```
                                        getVolume());
                }
            }
        }

        public void volumeDown() {
            if (isOn()) {
                if (getVolume() > MIN_VOLUME) {
                    volume--;
                    System.out.println("Volume turned down to level " +
                                        getVolume());
                }
            }
        }

    }
```

As you can see, the class enables the radio to be switched on and off, and provided it is switched on will enable the volume to be increased or decreased one level at a time, within the range 1 to 10[1].

Some of the vehicles also have electrically operated windows with simple up & down buttons, as modelled by the following `ElectricWindow` class[2].

```
    public class ElectricWindow {

        private boolean open;

        public ElectricWindow() {
            open = false;
            System.out.println("Window is closed");
        }

        public boolean isOpen() {
            return open;
        }

        public boolean isClosed() {
            return (! open);
        }

        public void openWindow() {
            if (isClosed()) {
                open = true;
                System.out.println("Window is now open");
            }
```

---

[1]The code to set the station frequency has been omitted.
[2]For simplicity the windows can only be either fully open or fully closed.

```
        }

    public void closeWindow() {
        if (isOpen()) {
            open = false;
            System.out.println("Window is now closed");
        }
    }

}
```

Each of the devices (the radio and the electric window) has separate controls, typically buttons, to manage their state. But suppose the Foobar Motor Company now wishes to introduce speech recognition to their top-of-the-range vehicles and have them perform as follows:

- *If the speech-recognition system is in "radio" mode, then if it hears the word "up" or "down" it adjusts the radio volume; or*

- *If the speech-recognition system is in "window" mode, then if it hears the word "up" or "down" it closes or opens the driver's door window.*

We therefore need the speech-recognition system to be able to handle either Radio objects or ElectricWindow objects, which are of course in completely separate hierarchies. We might also want it to handle other devices in the future, such as the vehicle's speed or the gearbox (e.g. upon hearing "up" it would increase the speed by 1mph or it would change to the next higher gear). For good object-oriented design we need to isolate the speech-recognition from the devices it controls, so it can cope with any device without directly knowing what they are.

The *Command* patterns allows us to uncouple an object making a request from the object that receives the request and performs the action, by means of a "middle-man" object known as a "command object".

In its simplest form, this requires us to create an interface (which we shall call Command) with one method:

```
public interface Command {
```

```
    public void execute();

}
```

We now need to create implementing classes for each action that we wish to take[1]. For example, to turn up the volume of the radio we can create a VolumeUpCommand class:

```
public class VolumeUpCommand implements Command {

    private Radio radio;

    public VolumeUpCommand(Radio radio) {
        this.radio = radio;
    }

    public void execute() {
        radio.volumeUp();
    }

}
```

The class simply takes a reference to a Radio object in its constructor and invokes its volumeUp() method whenever execute() is called.

We likewise need to create a VolumeDownCommand class for when the volume is to be reduced:

```
public class VolumeDownCommand implements Command {

    private Radio radio;

    public VolumeDownCommand(Radio radio) {
        this.radio = radio;
    }

    public void execute() {
        radio.volumeDown();
    }

}
```

---

[1]The *Command* pattern is sometimes known as the *Action* pattern.

Controlling an electric window's up and down movement is just as easy: this time we create classes implementing `Command` passing in a reference to an `ElectricWindow` object:

```
public class WindowUpCommand implements Command {

    private ElectricWindow window;

    public WindowUpCommand(ElectricWindow window) {
        this.window = window;
    }

    public void execute() {
        window.closeWindow();
    }


public class WindowDownCommand implements Command {

    private ElectricWindow window;

    public WindowDownCommand(ElectricWindow window) {
        this.window = window;
    }

    public void execute() {
        window.openWindow();
    }

}
```

We will now define a `SpeechRecogniser` class that only knows about `Command` objects – it knows nothing about radios or electric windows.

```
public class SpeechRecogniser {

    private Command upCommand, downCommand;

    public void setCommands(Command upCommand, Command downCommand) {
        this.upCommand = upCommand;
        this.downCommand = downCommand;
    }

    public void hearUpSpoken() {
        upCommand.execute();
    }

    public void hearDownSpoken() {
        downCommand.execute();
    }
}
```

We can view what we have created diagrammatically as follows:

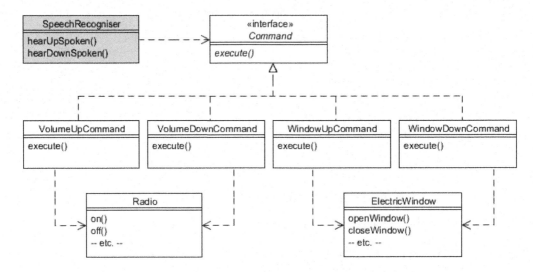

Figure 15.1 : Command pattern

Client programs can now create `Radio` and `ElectricWindow` instances, along with their respective `Command` instances. The command instances are then passed to the `SpeechRecogniser` object so it knows what to do.

We will first create a `Radio` and an `ElectricWindow` and their respective commands:

```
// Create a radio and its up/down command objects
Radio radio = new Radio();
radio.on();
Command volumeUpCommand = new VolumeUpCommand(radio);
Command volumeDownCommand = new VolumeDownCommand(radio);

// Create an electric window and its up/down command objects
ElectricWindow window = new ElectricWindow();
Command windowUpCommand = new WindowUpCommand(window);
Command windowDownCommand = new WindowDownCommand(window);
```

Now create a single `SpeechRecogniser` object and set it to control the radio:

```
// Create a speech recognition object
SpeechRecogniser speechRecogniser = new SpeechRecogniser();

// Control the radio
speechRecogniser.setCommands(volumeUpCommand, volumeDownCommand);
System.out.println("Speech recognition controlling the radio");
speechRecogniser.hearUpSpoken();
speechRecogniser.hearUpSpoken();
speechRecogniser.hearUpSpoken();
speechRecogniser.hearDownSpoken();
```

Now set the *same* `SpeechRecogniser` object to control the window instead:

```
// Control the electric window
speechRecogniser.setCommands(windowUpCommand, windowDownCommand);
System.out.println("Speech recognition will now control the window");
speechRecogniser.hearDownSpoken();
speechRecogniser.hearUpSpoken();
```

If you run all the above statements you should see output similar to this:

```
Radio now on, volume level 5
Window is closed
Speech recognition controlling the radio
Volume turned up to level 6
Volume turned up to level 7
Volume turned up to level 8
Volume turned down to level 7
Speech recognition will now control the window
Window is now open
Window is now closed
```

Typical uses of the Command Pattern

One of the most frequent uses of the *Command* pattern is in UI toolkits. These provide pre-built components like graphical buttons and menu items that cannot possibly know what needs to be done when clicked, because that is always specific to your application. In the Java libraries this is implemented through the `Action` interface's `actionPerformed()` method. Graphical applications often define both a menubar item and a toolbar icon that perform the same action (e.g. the `File | Open` menu item, and an

'Open' icon on a toolbar), where a single command object handles the action that is taken when either is selected.

Another common aspect of graphical applications is the provision of an "undo" mechanism. The *Command* pattern is used to accomplish this too; using the example in this chapter, we would add a method to the `Command` interface like this:

```
public interface Command {

    public void execute();
    public void undo();


}
```

Implementing classes then provide the code for the additional method to reverse the last action, as in this example for the `VolumeUpCommand` class:

```
public class VolumeUpCommand implements Command {

    private Radio radio;

    public VolumeUpCommand(Radio r) {
        radio = r;
    }

    public void execute() {
        radio.volumeUp();
    }

    public void undo() {
        radio.volumeDown();
    }


}
```

Most applications would be slightly more involved than the above example, in that you would need to store the state of the object prior to performing the code in the `execute()` method, enabling you to restore that state when `undo()` is called.

16. Interpreter

Type	Behavioural
Purpose	Given a language, define a representation for its grammar along with an interpreter that uses the representation to interpret sentences in the language.

The satellite-navigation systems fitted to some of the Foobar Motor Company's vehicles have a special feature that enables the user to enter a number of cities and let it calculate the most northerly, southerly, westerly or easterly, depending on which command string is entered. A sample command might look like this:

```
london edinburgh manchester southerly
```

The above would result in "London" being returned, being the most southerly of the three entered cities. You can even enter the command string like this:

```
london edinburgh manchester southerly aberdeen westerly
```

This would first determine that London was the most southerly and then use that result (London) and compare it to Aberdeen to tell you which of those two is the most westerly[1]. Any number of cities can be entered before each of the directional commands of "northerly", "southerly", "westerly" and "easterly".

You can think of the above command string consisting of the city names and directional keywords as forming a simple "language" that needs to be interpreted by the satellite-navigation software. The *Interpreter* pattern is

---

[1] It's Aberdeen.

an approach that helps to decipher these kinds of relatively simple languages.

Before looking at the pattern itself, we shall create a class named `City` which models the essential points of interest for our example, which is just the name of the city and its latitude and longitude:

```
public class City {

    private String name;
    private double latitude, longitude;

    public City(String name, double latitude, double longitude) {
        this.name = name;
        this.latitude = latitude;
        this.longitude = longitude;
    }

    public String getName() {
        return name;
    }

    public double getLatitude() {
        return latitude;
    }

    public double getLongitude() {
        return longitude;
    }

    public boolean equals(Object otherObject) {
        if (this == otherObject) return true;
        if (! (otherObject instanceof City)) return false;
        City otherCity = (City) otherObject;
        return getName().equals(otherCity.getName());
    }

    public int hashCode() {
        return getName().hashCode();
    }

    public String toString() {
        return getName();
    }

}
```

You will notice that for simplicity the latitude and longitude are stored as doubles. Also note that for the latitude positive values represent North and negative values represent South. Similarly, a positive longitude represents

East and negative values West. The example in this chapter only includes a small number of UK cities which are all Northern latitude and Western longitude, although any city should work should you wish to use your own.

The classes to interpret the language are structured as follows:

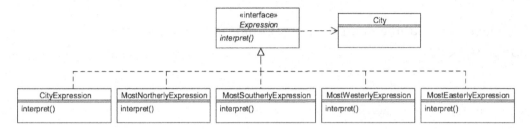

Figure 16.1 : Interpreter pattern

The *Interpreter* pattern resembles the *Composite* pattern in that it comprises an interface (or abstract class) with two types of concrete subclass; one type that represents the individual elements and the other type that represents repeating elements. We create one subclass to handle each type of element in the language.

The `Expression` interface is very simple, merely declaring an `interpret()` method that returns a `City` object:

```
public interface Expression {

    public City interpret();

}
```

The first concrete subclass we will look at is `CityExpression`, an instance of which will be created for each city name it recognises in the command string. All this class needs to do is store a reference to a `City` object and return it when `interpret()` is invoked:

```
public class CityExpression implements Expression {

    private City city;
```

```
    public CityExpression(City city) {
        this.city = city;
    }

    public City interpret() {
        return city;
    }
}
```

The classes to handle each of the commands (e.g. "northerly") are slightly more involved:

```
public class MostNortherlyExpression implements Expression {

    private List<Expression> expressions;

    public MostNortherlyExpression(List<Expression> expressions) {
        this.expressions = expressions;
    }

    public City interpret() {
        City resultingCity = new City("Nowhere", -999.9, -999.9);
        for (Expression currentExpression : expressions) {
            City currentCity = currentExpression.interpret();
            if (currentCity.getLatitude() >
                        resultingCity.getLatitude()) {
                resultingCity = currentCity;
            }
        }
        return resultingCity;
    }
}
```

The list of Expression objects passed to the constructor will be of the CityExpression type. The interpret() method loops through each of these to determine the most northerly, by comparing their latitude values.

The MostSoutherlyExpression class is very similar, merely changing the comparison:

```
public class MostSoutherlyExpression implements Expression {

    private List<Expression> expressions;

    public MostSoutherlyExpression(List<Expression> expressions) {
        this.expressions = expressions;
    }
```

```
    public City interpret() {
        City resultingCity = new City("Nowhere", 999.9, 999.9);
        for (Expression currentExpression : expressions) {
            City currentCity = currentExpression.interpret();
            if (currentCity.getLatitude() <
                    resultingCity.getLatitude()) {
                resultingCity = currentCity;
            }
        }
        return resultingCity;
    }
}
```

Likewise the `MostWesterlyExpression` and `MostEasterlyExpression` classes compute and return the appropriate `City`:

```
public class MostWesterlyExpression implements Expression {

    private List<Expression> expressions;

    public MostWesterlyExpression(List<Expression> expressions) {
        this.expressions = expressions;
    }

    public City interpret() {
        City resultingCity = new City("Nowhere", 999.9, 999.9);
        for (Expression currentExpression : expressions) {
            City currentCity = currentExpression.interpret();
            if (currentCity.getLongitude() <
                    resultingCity.getLongitude()) {
                resultingCity = currentCity;
            }
        }
        return resultingCity;
    }
}


public class MostEasterlyExpression implements Expression {

    private List<Expression> expressions;

    public MostEasterlyExpression(List<Expression> expressions) {
        this.expressions = expressions;
    }

    public City interpret() {
        City resultingCity = new City("Nowhere", -999.9, -999.9);
        for (Expression currentExpression : expressions) {
            City currentCity = currentExpression.interpret();
            if (currentCity.getLongitude() <
                    resultingCity.getLongitude()) {
                resultingCity = currentCity;
```

```
            }
        }
        return resultingCity;
    }
}
```

While the *Interpreter* pattern does not in itself cover the parsing of an expression, in practice we need to define a class to go through the command string (such as "london edinburgh manchester southerly") and create the appropriate `Expression` classes as we go along. These `Expression` classes are placed into a "syntax tree" which is normally implemented using a LIFO[1] stack. We shall therefore define a `DirectionalEvaluator` class to do this parsing, and set-up a small sample of UK cities:

```
public class DirectionalEvaluator {

    private Map<String, City> cities;

    public DirectionalEvaluator() {
        cities = new HashMap<String, City>();

        cities.put("aberdeen",
                new City("Aberdeen", 57.15, -2.15));
        cities.put("belfast",
                new City("Belfast", 54.62, -5.93));
        cities.put("birmingham",
                new City("Birmingham", 52.42, -1.92));
        cities.put("dublin",
                new City("Dublin", 53.33, -6.25));
        cities.put("edinburgh",
                new City("Edinburgh", 55.92, -3.02));
        cities.put("glasgow",
                new City("Glasgow", 55.83, -4.25));
        cities.put("london",
                new City("London", 51.53, -0.08));
        cities.put("liverpool",
                new City("Liverpool", 53.42, -3.0));
        cities.put("manchester",
                new City("Manchester", 53.5, -2.25));
        cities.put("southampton",
                new City("Southampton", 50.9, -1.38));
    }

    public City evaluate(String route) {
        // Define the syntax tree
        Stack<Expression> expressionStack = new Stack<Expression>();
```

---

[1]Last In First Out.

```java
        // Parse each token in route string
        for (String token : route.split(" ")) {
            // Is token a recognised city?
            if (cities.containsKey(token)) {
                City city = cities.get(token);
                expressionStack.push(new CityExpression(city));

            // Is token to find most northerly?
            } else if (token.equals("northerly")) {
                expressionStack.push
                        (new MostNortherlyExpression
                                (loadExpressions(expressionStack)));

            // Is token to find most southerly?
            } else if (token.equals("southerly")) {
                expressionStack.push
                        (new MostSoutherlyExpression
                                (loadExpressions(expressionStack)));

            // Is token to find most westerly?
            } else if (token.equals("westerly")) {
                expressionStack.push
                        (new MostWesterlyExpression
                                (loadExpressions(expressionStack)));

            // Is token to find most easterly?
            } else if (token.equals("easterly")) {
                expressionStack.push
                        (new MostEasterlyExpression
                                (loadExpressions(expressionStack)));
            }
        }

        // Resulting value
        return expressionStack.pop().interpret();
    }

    private List<Expression> loadExpressions
            (Stack<Expression> expressionStack) {

        List<Expression> expressions =
                new ArrayList<Expression>();
        while(! expressionStack.empty()) {
            expressions.add(expressionStack.pop());
        }
        return expressions;
    }

}
```

Within the `evaluate()` method, when the parser detects a directional command (such as "northerly") it removes the cities on the stack and passes them along with the command back to the stack.

> Note that the use above of if...else... statements has been used simply so that the chapter concentrates on the *Interpreter* pattern. A better approach would be to use a separate pattern to handle each token such as that defined in *Chain of Responsibility*.

Now all that remains is for our client programs to utilise the DirectionalEvaluator passing the command to interpret:

```java
// Create the evaluator
DirectionalEvaluator evaluator = new DirectionalEvaluator();

// This should output "London"...
System.out.println(evaluator.evaluate
        ("london edinburgh manchester southerly"));

// This should output "Aberdeen"...
System.out.println(evaluator.evaluate
        ("london edinburgh manchester southerly aberdeen westerly"));
```

17. Iterator

Type	Behavioural
Purpose	Provide a way to access the elements of an aggregate object sequentially without exposing its underlying representation.

The Foobar Motor Company wanted to produce a brochure listing their range of vehicles for sale and allocated the task to two separate programmers, one to provide the range of cars and the other to provide the range of vans.

The programmer that coded the CarRange class decided to internally store the range using a List object from the Java collections (specifically an ArrayList):

```
public class CarRange {

    private List<Vehicle> cars;

    public CarRange() {
        cars = new ArrayList<Vehicle>();

        cars.add(new Saloon(new StandardEngine(1300)));
        cars.add(new Saloon(new StandardEngine(1600)));
        cars.add(new Coupe(new StandardEngine(2000)));
        cars.add(new Sport(new TurboEngine(2500)));
    }

    public List<Vehicle> getRange() {
        return cars;
    }

}
```

You can see from the above that the programmer provided a getRange() method that returns the List collection object.

The other programmer decided to store the vans in an array when writing the VanRange class, and therefore his version of getRange() returns an array of vehicles:

```
public class VanRange {

    private Vehicle[] vans;

    public VanRange() {
        vans = new Vehicle[3];

        vans[0] = new BoxVan(new StandardEngine(1600));
        vans[1] = new BoxVan(new StandardEngine(2000));
        vans[2] = new Pickup(new TurboEngine(2200));
    }

    public Vehicle[] getRange() {
        return vans;
    }

}
```

The problem with this is that the internal representation in both of these classes has been exposed to outside objects. A better approach would be for each of the CarRange and VanRange classes to provide an Iterator object so that as well as being consistent, the internal representation would not need to be exposed.

The Java Iterator interface is an implementation of the *Iterator* pattern, and looks like this (it is in the java.util package):

```
public interface Iterator<E> {

    public boolean hasNext();
    public E next();
    public void remove();

}
```

- The hasNext() method returns true if another item exists;

- The next() method returns the next item;

- The remove() method removes the last returned item.

For lists, a subclass of `Iterator` called `ListIterator` provides some additional methods.

Another Java interface called `Iterable` (which is in `java.lang`) can be implemented by classes that define a method called `iterator()` that returns an `Iterator` object:

```
public interface Iterable<T> {

    public Iterator<T> iterator();

}
```

Armed with this knowledge we can now modify our `CarRange` class to implement the `Iterable` interface and provide the new required method (code changes in bold):

```
public class CarRange implements Iterable<Vehicle> {

    private List<Vehicle> cars;

    public CarRange() {
        cars = new ArrayList<Vehicle>();

        cars.add(new Saloon(new StandardEngine(1300)));
        cars.add(new Saloon(new StandardEngine(1600)));
        cars.add(new Coupe(new StandardEngine(2000)));
        cars.add(new Sport(new TurboEngine(2500)));
    }

    public List<Vehicle> getRange() {
        return cars;
    }

    public Iterator<Vehicle> iterator() {
        return cars.listIterator();
    }

}
```

The `VanRange` class can also be changed along similar lines, this time converting the internal array into an `Iterator`:

```
public class VanRange implements Iterable<Vehicle> {
```

```
    private Vehicle[] vans;

    public VanRange() {
        vans = new Vehicle[3];

        Engine onePointSix = new StandardEngine(1600);
        Engine twoLitreTurbo = new TurboEngine(2000);

        vans[0] = new BoxVan(new StandardEngine(1600));
        vans[1] = new BoxVan(new StandardEngine(2000));
        vans[2] = new Pickup(new TurboEngine(2200));
    }

    public Vehicle[] getRange() {
        return vans;
    }

    public Iterator<Vehicle> iterator() {
        return Arrays.asList(vans).listIterator();
    }

}
```

Now we can process both cars and vans in a consistent manner:

```
System.out.println("=== Our Cars ===");
CarRange carRange = new CarRange();
printIterator(carRange.iterator());
System.out.println("=== Our Vans ===");
VanRange vanRange = new VanRange();
printIterator(vanRange.iterator());

public void printIterator(Iterator iter) {
    while (iter.hasNext()) {
        System.out.println(iter.next());
    }
}
```

The 'for-each' loop

Several of the other chapters in this book have made use of the *for-each*
construct introduced with Java 5. By implementing the Iterable interface
your own classes can make use of this, providing a clean alternative to the
above, as follows:

```
System.out.println("=== Our Cars ===");
CarRange carRange = new CarRange();
for (Vehicle currentVehicle : carRange.getRange()) {
```

```
        System.out.println(currentVehicle);
}

System.out.println("=== Our Vans ===");
VanRange vanRange = new VanRange();
for (Vehicle currentVehicle : vanRange.getRange()) {
        System.out.println(currentVehicle);
}
```

18. Mediator

Type	Behavioural
Purpose	Define an object that encapsulates how a set of objects interact. *Mediator* promotes loose coupling by keeping objects from referring to each other explicitly, and it lets you vary their interaction independently.

The Foobar Motor Company is looking to the future when vehicles can drive themselves. This, of course, would entail the various components (ignition, gearbox, accelerator and brakes, etc.) being controlled together and interacting in various ways. For example:

- *Until the ignition is switched on, the gearbox, accelerator and brakes do not operate (we will assume the parking brake is in effect);*

- *When accelerating, the brakes should be disabled;*

- *When braking the accelerator should be disabled;*

- *The appropriate gear should be engaged dependent upon the speed of the vehicle.*

And all this should happen automatically so the driver can just enjoy the view! (We will assume the vehicle can sense its position so as to avoid crashes, etc.).

We will naturally create Java classes to model the individual components, so there will be an `Ignition` class, a `Gearbox` class, an `Accelerator` class and a `Brake` class. But we can also see that there are some complex interactions between them, and yet one of our core object-oriented design principles is to keep classes loosely-coupled.

The *Mediator* pattern helps to solve this through the definition of a separate class (the mediator) that knows about the individual component classes and takes responsibility for managing their interaction. The component classes also each know about the mediator class, but this is the only coupling they have. For our example, we will call the mediator class EngineManagementSystem.

We can see the connections diagrammatically below:

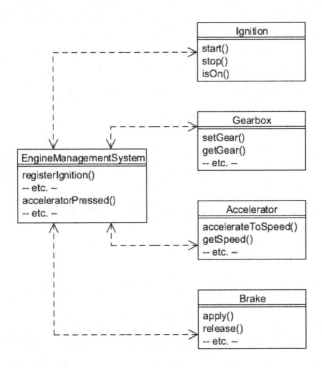

Figure 18.1 : Mediator pattern

The two-way communication is achieved via each of the component classes' constructors, in that they each accept a reference to the mediator object (so they can send messages to it) and register themselves with the mediator (so they can receive messages from it). But each component class has no knowledge of any other component class; they only know about the mediator.

We can see this by looking at the `Ignition` class:

```
public class Ignition {

    private EngineManagementSystem mediator;
    private boolean on;

    // Constructor accepts mediator as an argument
    public Ignition(EngineManagementSystem mediator) {
        this.mediator = mediator;
        on = false;

        // Register back with the mediator...
        mediator.registerIgnition(this);
    }

    public void start() {
        on = true;
        mediator.ignitionTurnedOn();
        System.out.println("Ignition turned on");
    }

    public void stop() {
        on = false;
        mediator.ignitionTurnedOff();
        System.out.println("Ignition turned off");
    }

    public boolean isOn() {
        return on;
    }

}
```

Note how the constructor establishes the two-way communication, and then how methods that perform events notify the mediator of those events.

The `Gearbox` class applies the same principles:

```
public class Gearbox {

    public enum Gear {NEUTRAL,
                      FIRST, SECOND, THIRD, FOURTH, FIFTH,
                      REVERSE};

    private EngineManagementSystem mediator;
    private boolean enabled;
    private Gear currentGear;

    public Gearbox(EngineManagementSystem mediator) {
        this.mediator = mediator;
        enabled = false;
```

```
            currentGear = Gear.NEUTRAL;
            mediator.registerGearbox(this);
        }

    public void enable() {
            enabled = true;
            mediator.gearboxEnabled();
            System.out.println("Gearbox enabled");
        }

    public void disable() {
            enabled = false;
            mediator.gearboxDisabled();
            System.out.println("Gearbox disabled");
        }

    public boolean isEnabled() {
            return enabled;
        }

    public void setGear(Gear g) {
            if ((isEnabled()) && (getGear() != g)) {
                currentGear = g;
                mediator.gearChanged();
                System.out.println("Now in " + getGear() + " gear");
            }
        }
    public Gear getGear() {
            return currentGear;
        }

    }
```

The `Accelerator` and `Brake` classes follow a similar process:

```
public class Accelerator {

    private EngineManagementSystem mediator;
    private boolean enabled;
    private int speed;

    public Accelerator(EngineManagementSystem mediator) {
        this.mediator = mediator;
        enabled = false;
        speed = 0;
        mediator.registerAccelerator(this);
    }

    public void enable() {
        enabled = true;
        mediator.acceleratorEnabled();
        System.out.println("Accelerator enabled");
    }
```

```java
    public void disable() {
        enabled = false;
        mediator.acceleratorDisabled();
        System.out.println("Accelerator disabled");
    }

    public boolean isEnabled() {
        return enabled;
    }

    public void accelerateToSpeed(int speed) {
        if (isEnabled()) {
            this.speed = speed;
            mediator.acceleratorPressed();
            System.out.println("Speed now " + getSpeed());
        }
    }

    public int getSpeed() {
        return speed;
    }

}


public class Brake {

    private EngineManagementSystem mediator;
    private boolean enabled;
    private boolean applied;

    public Brake(EngineManagementSystem mediator) {
        this.mediator = mediator;
        enabled = false;
        applied = false;
        mediator.registerBrake(this);
    }

    public void enable() {
        enabled = true;
        mediator.brakeEnabled();
        System.out.println("Brakes enabled");
    }

    public void disable() {
        enabled = false;
        mediator.brakeDisabled();
        System.out.println("Brakes disabled");
    }

    public boolean isEnabled() {
        return enabled;
    }

    public void apply() {
        if (isEnabled()) {
```

```
                applied = true;
                mediator.brakePressed();
                System.out.println("Now braking");
            }
        }
    }

    public void release() {
        if (isEnabled()) {
            applied = false;
        }
    }

}
```

So we now need the `EngineManagementSystem` class to serve as the mediator. This will hold a reference to each of the component classes with methods enabling their registration with the mediator. It also has methods to handle the interaction between the various components when particular events occur:

```
public class EngineManagementSystem {

    private Ignition ignition;
    private Gearbox gearbox;
    private Accelerator accelerator;
    private Brake brake;

    private int currentSpeed;

    public EngineManagementSystem() {
        currentSpeed = 0;
    }


    // Methods that enable registration with this mediator...

    public void registerIgnition(Ignition ignition) {
        this.ignition = ignition;
    }

    public void registerGearbox(Gearbox gearbox) {
        this.gearbox = gearbox;
    }

    public void registerAccelerator(Accelerator accelerator) {
        this.accelerator = accelerator;
    }

    public void registerBrake(Brake brake) {
        this.brake = brake;
    }
```

```java
// Methods that handle object interactions...

public void ignitionTurnedOn() {
    gearbox.enable();
    accelerator.enable();
    brake.enable();
}

public void ignitionTurnedOff() {
    gearbox.disable();
    accelerator.disable();
    brake.disable();
}

public void gearboxEnabled() {
    System.out.println("EMS now controlling the gearbox");
}

public void gearboxDisabled() {
    System.out.println("EMS no longer controlling the gearbox");
}

public void gearChanged() {
    System.out.println
            ("EMS disengaging revs while gear changing");
}

public void acceleratorEnabled() {
    System.out.println
            ("EMS now controlling the accelerator");
}

public void acceleratorDisabled() {
    System.out.println
            ("EMS no longer controlling the accelerator");
}

public void acceleratorPressed() {
    brake.disable();
    while (currentSpeed < accelerator.getSpeed()) {

        currentSpeed ++;
        System.out.println
                ("Speed currently " + currentSpeed);

        // Set gear according to speed...
        if (currentSpeed <= 10) {
            gearbox.setGear(Gearbox.Gear.FIRST);

        } else if (currentSpeed <= 20) {
            gearbox.setGear(Gearbox.Gear.SECOND);

        } else if (currentSpeed <= 30) {
            gearbox.setGear(Gearbox.Gear.THIRD);

        } else if (currentSpeed <= 50) {
            gearbox.setGear(Gearbox.Gear.FOURTH);
```

```
            } else {
                gearbox.setGear(Gearbox.Gear.FIFTH);
            }
        }
        brake.enable();
    }

    public void brakeEnabled() {
        System.out.println("EMS now controlling the brakes");
    }

    public void brakeDisabled() {
        System.out.println("EMS no longer controlling the brakes");
    }

    public void brakePressed() {
        accelerator.disable();
        currentSpeed = 0;
    }

    public void brakeReleased() {
        gearbox.setGear(Gearbox.Gear.FIRST);
        accelerator.enable();
    }

}
```

Common uses

A common use of the *Mediator* pattern is to manage the interaction of graphical components on a dialog. This frequently involves controlling when buttons, text fields, etc. should be enabled or disabled, or for passing data between components.

Note that it may be possible to reduce the coupling further by using the *Observer* pattern in place of *Mediator*. This would mean that the component classes (i.e. Ignition, etc.) would not need to hold a reference to a mediator but would instead fire events. The EngineManagementSystem class would then be an observer of the component classes and would still be able to invoke messages on them.

19. Memento

Type	Behavioural
Purpose	Without violating encapsulation, capture and externalise an object's internal state so that it can be restored to this state later.

The Foobar Motor Company's vehicles naturally have a speedometer mounted on the dashboard, which not only records the current speed but also the previous speed. There is now a requirement for the state to be stored externally at periodic intervals (so that it could, for example, be integrated into a tachograph for goods vehicles).

However, one of the instance variables in the `Speedometer` class does not have a getter method, but to adhere to encapsulation and data-hiding principles it is correctly declared to be `private`. We also want to adhere to the principle that a class should not have multiple responsibilities, so don't want to also have to build in a state save & restore mechanism into the class. So how can we capture the state of the object?

This chapter will present two different approaches, each having its advantages and disadvantages. In both cases, we make use of a separate class that performs the state saving and restoration, which we shall call `SpeedometerMemento`. This class takes a reference to the `Speedometer` object that needs to be externalised:

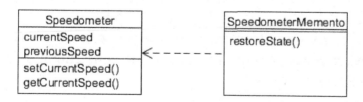

Figure 19.1 : Memento pattern

Approach 1 – using package-private visibility

When the access modifier is omitted from class members it takes on 'package-private' visibility[1]. This means it is only accessible to other classes in the same package, so is thus slightly more open than `private` visibility but not as much as `protected` (subclasses in different packages will be unable to access). Therefore we can place the `Speedometer` class into a package where we limit what other classes exist there, which in our case will just be `SpeedometerMemento`.

Here is the very simple `Speedometer` class:

```
package mementosubpackage;

public class Speedometer {

    // Normal private visibility but has accessor method...
    private int currentSpeed;

    // package-private visibility and no accessor method...
    int previousSpeed;

    public Speedometer() {
        currentSpeed = 0;
        previousSpeed = 0;
    }

    public void setCurrentSpeed(int speed) {
        previousSpeed = currentSpeed;
        currentSpeed = speed;
    }

    public int getCurrentSpeed() {
        return currentSpeed;
    }

}
```

The `SpeedometerMemento` class exists in the same package. It saves the state of the passed in `Speedometer` object in the constructor and defines a method to restore that state:

```
package mementosubpackage;

public class SpeedometerMemento {
```

---

[1]Also known as 'default' visibility.

```
        private Speedometer speedometer;

        private int copyOfCurrentSpeed;
        private int copyOfPreviousSpeed;

        public SpeedometerMemento(Speedometer speedometer) {
            this.speedometer = speedometer;
            copyOfCurrentSpeed = speedometer.getCurrentSpeed();
            copyOfPreviousSpeed = speedometer.previousSpeed;
        }

        public void restoreState() {
            speedometer.setCurrentSpeed(copyOfCurrentSpeed);
            speedometer.previousSpeed = copyOfPreviousSpeed;
        }

    }
```

Note that the accessor method `getCurrentSpeed()` was used for the `currentSpeed` instance variable but the `previousSpeed` variable had to be accessed directly, which is possible because the memento exists in the same package.

We can test the memento with this code:

```
Speedometer speedo = new Speedometer();

speedo.setCurrentSpeed(50);
speedo.setCurrentSpeed(100);
System.out.println("Current speed: " + speedo.getCurrentSpeed());
System.out.println("Previous speed: " + speedo.previousSpeed);

// Save the state of 'speedo'...
SpeedometerMemento memento = new SpeedometerMemento(speedo);

// Change the state of 'speedo'...
speedo.setCurrentSpeed(80);
System.out.println("After setting to 80...");
System.out.println("Current speed: " + speedo.getCurrentSpeed());
System.out.println("Previous speed: " + speedo.previousSpeed);

// Restore the state of 'speedo'...
System.out.println("Now restoring state...");
memento.restoreState();
System.out.println("Current speed: " + speedo.getCurrentSpeed());
System.out.println("Previous speed: " + speedo.previousSpeed);
```

Running the above results in the following output:

```
Current speed: 100
Previous speed: 50

After setting to 80...
Current speed: 80
Previous speed: 100

Now restoring state...
Current speed: 100
Previous speed: 50
```

The main disadvantage of this approach is that you either have to put the pair of classes in their own special package or accept that other classes in the package they are in will have direct access to the instance variables.

Approach 2 – object serialization

This approach allows you to make all the instance variables `private`, thus regaining full encapsulation. The `Speedometer` class has been modified for this and now includes a `getPreviousSpeed()` method, though this is purely to help us test the memento; it's not required by this approach. The class has also been changed to implement the `Serializable` interface (changes marked in bold):

```
public class Speedometer implements Serializable {

    private int currentSpeed;
    private int previousSpeed;

    public Speedometer() {
        currentSpeed = 0;
        previousSpeed = 0;
    }

    public void setCurrentSpeed(int speed) {
        previousSpeed = currentSpeed;
        currentSpeed = speed;
    }

    public int getCurrentSpeed() {
        return currentSpeed;
    }
```

```
    // Only defined to help testing...
    public int getPreviousSpeed() {
        return previousSpeed;
    }

}
```

The SpeedometerMemento class now uses object serialization for the state saving and restoration:

```
public class SpeedometerMemento {

    public SpeedometerMemento(Speedometer speedometer) throws
                    IOException {
        // Serialize...
        File speedometerFile = new File("speedometer.ser");
        oos = new ObjectOutputStream(
                new BufferedOutputStream(
                    new FileOutputStream(speedometerFile)));
        oos.writeObject(speedometer);
        oos.close();
    }

    public Speedometer restoreState() throws IOException,
                                        ClassNotFoundException {
        // Deserialize...
        File speedometerFile = new File("speedometer.ser");
        ois = new ObjectInputStream(
                new BufferedInputStream(
                    new FileInputStream(speedometerFile)));
        Speedometer speedo = (Speedometer) ois.readObject();
        ois.close();
        return speedo;
    }

}
```

We can check that this achieves the same as the first approach, the only difference being that the restoreState() method now returns the restored object reference:

```
Speedometer speedo = new Speedometer();

speedo.setCurrentSpeed(50);
speedo.setCurrentSpeed(100);
System.out.println("Current speed: " + speedo.getCurrentSpeed());
System.out.println("Previous speed: " + speedo. getPreviousSpeed());

// Save the state of 'speedo'...
SpeedometerMemento memento = new SpeedometerMemento(speedo);
```

```
// Change the state of 'speedo'...
speedo.setCurrentSpeed(80);
System.out.println("After setting to 80...");
System.out.println("Current speed: " + speedo.getCurrentSpeed());
System.out.println("Previous speed: " + speedo.getPreviousSpeed());

// Restore the state of 'speedo'...
System.out.println("Now restoring state...");
speedo = memento.restoreState();
System.out.println("Current speed: " + speedo.getCurrentSpeed());
System.out.println("Previous speed: " + speedo.getPreviousSpeed());
```

Running the above should result in the same output as shown for the first approach. The main disadvantage of this approach is that writing to and reading from a disk file is much slower. Note also that while we have been able to make all fields `private` again, it might still be possible for someone who gained access to the serialized file to use a hex editor to read or change the data.

20. Observer

Type	Behavioural
Purpose	Define a one-to-many dependency between objects so that when one object changes its state, all its dependants are notified and updated automatically.

The Foobar Motor Company has decided that an alert should sound to the driver whenever a certain speed is exceeded. They also envisage that other things may need to happen depending upon the current speed (such as an automatic gearbox selecting the appropriate gear to match the speed). But they realise the need to keep objects loosely-coupled, so naturally don't wish the Speedometer class to have any direct knowledge of speed monitors or automatic gearboxes (or any other future class that might be interested in the speed a vehicle is travelling).

The *Observer* pattern enables a loose-coupling to be established between a 'subject' (the object that is of interest; Speedometer on our example) and its 'observers' (any other class that needs to be kept informed when interesting stuff happens).

Because this is a very common need in object-oriented systems, the Java libraries already contains mechanisms that enable the pattern to be implemented. One of these is by utilising the Observable class and the Observer interface[1]:

---

[1]These both reside in the java.util package.

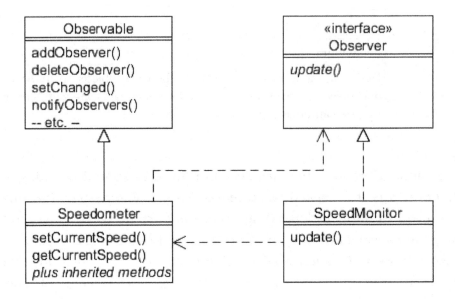

Figure 20.1 : Observer pattern

The 'subject' (Speedometer) can have multiple observers (which can in fact be any class that implements the Observer interface, not just SpeedMonitor objects).

The Speedometer class looks like this[1]:

```
public class Speedometer extends Observable {

    private int currentSpeed;

    public Speedometer() {
        speed = 0;
    }

    public void setCurrentSpeed(int speed) {
        currentSpeed = speed;

        // Tell all observers so they know speed has changed...
        setChanged();
```

---

[1]Unlike the version in the *Memento* pattern chapter, there is no variable to record the previous speed as it is irrelevant to this example.

```
            notifyObservers();
    }

    public int getCurrentSpeed() {
        return currentSpeed;
    }

}
```

The `Speedometer` class extends `java.util.Observable` and thus inherits for our convenience its methods concerned with the registration and notification of observers. For our example, whenever the speed has changed we invoke the inherited `setChanged()` and `notifyObservers()`[1] methods which takes care of the notifications for us.

The `SpeedMonitor` class implements the `java.util.Observer` interface and has the appropriate code for its required method `update()`:

```
public class SpeedMonitor implements Observer {

    public static final int SPEED_TO_ALERT = 70;

    public void update(Observable obs, Object obj) {
        Speedometer speedo = (Speedometer) obs;
        if (speedo.getCurrentSpeed() > SPEED_TO_ALERT) {
            System.out.println("** ALERT ** Driving too fast! (" +
                            speedo.getCurrentSpeed() + ")");
        } else {
            System.out.println("... nice and steady ... (" +
                            speedo.getCurrentSpeed() + ")");
        }
    }

}
```

Client programs simply pass a `SpeedMonitor` reference to an instance of `Speedometer`:

```
// Create a monitor...
SpeedMonitor monitor = new SpeedMonitor();

// Create a speedometer and register the monitor to it...
Speedometer speedo = new Speedometer();
```

---

[1]You can optionally pass an `Object` argument to `notifyObservers()`.

```
speedo.addObserver(monitor);

// Drive at different speeds...
speedo.setCurrentSpeed(50);
speedo.setCurrentSpeed(70);
speedo.setCurrentSpeed(40);
speedo.setCurrentSpeed(100);
speedo.setCurrentSpeed(69);
```

Running the above will result in the following output:

```
... nice and steady ... (50)
... nice and steady ... (70)
... nice and steady ... (40)
** ALERT ** Driving too fast! (100)
... nice and steady ... (69)
```

The real power behind the *Observer* pattern is that any type of class can now become a monitor provided they implement the `Observer` interface, and without requiring any changes to be made to `Speedometer`. Let's create a simulation of an automatic gearbox:

```java
public class AutomaticGearbox implements Observer {

    public void update(Observable obs, Object obj) {
        Speedometer speedo = (Speedometer) obs;

        if (speedo.getCurrentSpeed() <= 10) {
            System.out.println("Now in first gear");

        } else if (speedo.getCurrentSpeed() <= 20) {
            System.out.println("Now in second gear");

        } else if (speedo.getCurrentSpeed() <= 30) {
            System.out.println("Now in third gear");

        } else {
            System.out.println("Now in fourth gear");
        }
    }

}
```

Our client program can now just add this as an additional observer and get notifications of speed changes as well:

```java
speedo.addObserver(new AutomaticGearbox());
```

An alternative approach using events & listeners

The inherited code that makes `Observable` classes work does have an obvious downside – if your subject class already extends another class then you can't extend it as well, since Java only supports single inheritance (of classes). However, providing your own implementation is fairly straightforward, and here we will make use of an alternative approach provided by the Java libraries using 'events' and 'listeners'.

The first thing we shall do is separate out the events that can occur into a class called `SpeedometerEvent` that extends `java.util.EventObject`:

```
public class SpeedometerEvent extends EventObject {

    private int speed;

    public SpeedometerEvent(Object source, int speed) {
        super(source);
        this.speed = speed;
    }

    public int getSpeed() {
        return speed;
    }

}
```

The only event of interest is when the speed changes. The inherited `EventObject` class provides a `getSource()` method so listeners will be able to tell the exact object that gave rise to the event, if they need to know it for some reason.

Going hand-in-hand with `SpeedometerEvent` is an interface we shall define called `SpeedometerListener`, which extends the `java.util.EventListener` interface[1]:

```
public interface SpeedometerListener extends EventListener {
```

---

[1]This is a tagging interface that has no methods defined but should be extended by listeners.

```
      public void speedChanged(SpeedometerEvent event);

}
```

All classes that implement `SpeedometerListener` will need to provide appropriate code for the `speedChanged()` method. They can get any required data through the `SpeedometerEvent` reference passed in the argument. Note that our simple example only defines the one method, but it is common to have several methods that each notify a different piece of state that has changed.

The `Speedometer` class will now be modified to no longer extend `java.util.Obervable` and to instead handle listener registration and notification internally:

```
   public class Speedometer {

       private int currentSpeed;
       private List<SpeedometerListener> listeners;

       public Speedometer() {
           currentSpeed= 0;
           listeners = new ArrayList<SpeedometerListener>();
       }

       public void setCurrentSpeed(int speed) {
           currentSpeed = speed;

           // Tell all observers so they know speed has changed...
           fireSpeedChanged();
       }

       public int getCurrentSpeed() {
           return currentSpeed;
       }

       public void addSpeedometerListener(SpeedometerListener obj) {
           listeners.add(obj);
       }

       public void removeSpeedometerListener(SpeedometerListener obj) {
           listeners.remove(obj);
       }

       protected void fireSpeedChanged() {
           SpeedometerEvent speedEvent =
```

```
                new SpeedometerEvent(this, getCurrentSpeed());

        for (SpeedometerListener eachListener : listeners) {
            eachListener.speedChanged(speedEvent);
        }
    }

}
```

Note the use of an `ArrayList` to maintain the list of listeners, along with methods to add and remove them and loop through them when an `SpeedometerEvent` needs to be sent.

The `SpeedMonitor` class is our listener and now needs to implement the `SpeedometerListener` interface instead of `java.util.Observable`:

```
public class SpeedMonitor implements SpeedometerListener {

    public static final int SPEED_TO_ALERT = 70;

    public void speedChanged(SpeedometerEvent event) {
        if (event.getSpeed() > SPEED_TO_ALERT) {
            System.out.println("** ALERT ** Driving too fast! (" +
                                        event.getSpeed() + ")");
        } else {
            System.out.println("... nice and steady ... (" +
                                        event.getSpeed() + ")");
        }
    }

}
```

Our client program is almost identical to before, the only change being a different method name when registering the listener:

```
// Create a listener
SpeedMonitor monitor = new SpeedMonitor();

// Create a speedometer and register the monitor to it...
Speedometer speedo = new Speedometer();
speedo.addSpeedometerListener(monitor);

// Drive at different speeds...
speedo.setCurrentSpeed(50);
speedo.setCurrentSpeed(70);
speedo.setCurrentSpeed(40);
speedo.setCurrentSpeed(100);
speedo.setCurrentSpeed(69);
```

If your classes are JavaBeans then the Java libraries also supply a `PropertyChangeEvent` class and `PropertyChangeListener` interface that follow a similar approach.

21. State

Type	Behavioural
Purpose	Allow an object to alter its behaviour when its internal state changes. The object will appear to change its class.

The Foobar Motor Company's vehicles each have a digital clock fitted that displays the current date and time. These values will need to be reset from time to time (such as after a change of battery) and this is accomplished by means of a particular knob on the dashboard. When the knob is initially pressed, the 'year' value can be set. Turning the knob to the left (i.e. anti-clockwise) causes the previous year to be show, whereas turning it to the right goes forward one year. When the knob is pressed again the year value becomes 'set' and the set-up process then automatically allows the month value to be set, also by making appropriate left or right movements with the knob.

This process continues for the day of the month, the hour and the minute. The following table summarises the flow of events:

User Action	What Happens
Push knob	Clock goes into 'setup' mode for setting **year**
Rotate knob left	1 is deducted from the **year** value
Rotate knob right	1 is added to the **year** value
Push knob	Year now set and automatically transitions into **month** set-up
Rotate knob left	1 is deducted from the **month** value
Rotate knob right	1 is added to the **month** value
Push knob	Month now set and automatically transitions into **day** set-up
Rotate knob left	1 is deducted from the **day** value
Rotate knob right	1 is added to the **day** value

Push knob	Day now set and automatically transitions into **hour** set-up
Rotate knob left	1 is deducted from the **hour** value
Rotate knob right	1 is added to the **hour** value
Push knob	Hour now set and automatically transitions into **minute** set-up
Rotate knob left	1 is deducted from the **minute** value
Rotate knob right	1 is added to the **minute** value
Push knob	Minute now set and automatically transitions for into '**finished**' mode
Push knob	Displays set date & time

From the above steps it is clear that different parts of the date & time get set when the knob is turned or pressed, and that there are transitions between those parts. A naive approach when coding a class to accomplish this would be to have a 'mode' variable and then a series of `if...else...` statements in each method, which might look like this:

```
// *** DON'T DO THIS! ***
public void rotateKnobLeft() {
    if (mode == YEAR_MODE) {
        year--;
    else if (mode == MONTH_MODE) {
        month--;
    else if (mode == DAY_MODE) {
        day--;
    else if (mode == HOUR_MODE) {
        hour--;
    else if (mode == MINUTE_MODE) {
        minute--;
}
```

The problem with code such as the above is that the `if...else...` conditions would have to be repeated in each action method (i.e. `rotateKnobRight()`, `pushKnob()`, etc.). Apart from making the code look unwieldy it also becomes hard to maintain, as if for example we now need to record seconds we would need to change multiple parts of the class.

The *State* pattern enables a hierarchy to be established that allows for state transitions such as necessitated by our clock setting example. We will create a ClockSetup class that initiates the states through the interface ClockSetupState, which has an implementing class for each individual state:

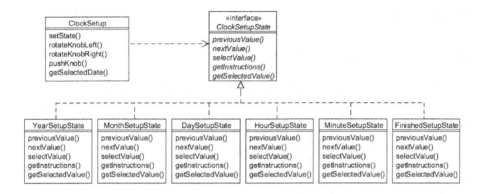

Figure 21.1 : State pattern

The ClockSetupState interface defines methods for handling changes to the state, plus methods that can provide user instructions and return the actual selected value:

```
public interface ClockSetupState {

    public void previousValue();
    public void nextValue();
    public void selectValue();

    public String getInstructions();
    public int getSelectedValue();

}
```

Looking first at YearSetupState, you will notice that it takes a reference to a ClockSetup object in the constructor (which is known in the language of design patterns as its 'context') and manages the setting of the year. Note in particular in the selectValue() method how it transitions internally to a different state:

```
public class YearSetupState implements ClockSetupState {

    private ClockSetup clockSetup;
    private int year;

    public YearSetupState(ClockSetup clockSetup) {
        this.clockSetup = clockSetup;
        year = Calendar.getInstance().get(Calendar.YEAR);
    }

    public void previousValue() {
        year--;
    }

    public void nextValue() {
        year++;
    }

    public void selectValue() {
        System.out.println("Year set to " + year);
        clockSetup.setState
                    (clockSetup.getMonthSetupState());
    }

    public String getInstructions() {
        return "Please set the year...";
    }

    public int getSelectedValue() {
        return year;
    }

}
```

The other date & time state classes follow a similar process, each transitioning to the next appropriate state when required:

```
public class MonthSetupState implements ClockSetupState {

    private ClockSetup clockSetup;
    private int month;

    public MonthSetupState(ClockSetup clockSetup) {
        this.clockSetup = clockSetup;
        month = Calendar.getInstance().get(Calendar.MONTH);
    }

    public void previousValue() {
        if (month > 0) {
            month--;
        }
    }

    public void nextValue() {
```

```java
        if (month < 11) {
            month++;
        }
    }

    public void selectValue() {
        System.out.println("Month set to " + month);
        clockSetup.setState
                (clockSetup.getDaySetupState());
    }

    public String getInstructions() {
        return "Please set the month...";
    }

    public int getSelectedValue() {
        return month;
    }

}


public class DaySetupState implements ClockSetupState {

    private ClockSetup clockSetup;
    private int day;

    public DaySetupState(ClockSetup clockSetup) {
        this.clockSetup = clockSetup;
        day = Calendar.getInstance().get(Calendar.DAY_OF_MONTH);
    }

    public void previousValue() {
        if (day > 1) {
            day--;
        }
    }

    public void nextValue() {
        if (day < Calendar.getInstance()
                    .getActualMaximum(Calendar.DAY_OF_MONTH) {
            day++;
        }
    }

    public void selectValue() {
        System.out.println("Day set to " + day);
        clockSetup.setState
                (clockSetup.getHourSetupState());
    }

    public String getInstructions() {
        return "Please set the day...";
    }

    public int getSelectedValue() {
```

```java
                return day;
        }

    }



    public class HourSetupState implements ClockSetupState {

        private ClockSetup clockSetup;
        private int hour;

        public HourSetupState(ClockSetup clockSetup) {
            this.clockSetup = clockSetup;
            hour = Calendar.getInstance().get(Calendar.HOUR);
        }

        public void previousValue() {
            if (hour > 0) {
                hour--;
            }
        }

        public void nextValue() {
            if (hour < 23) {
                hour++;
            }
        }

        public void selectValue() {
            System.out.println("Hour set to " + hour);
            clockSetup.setState
                    (clockSetup.getMinuteSetupState());
        }

        public String getInstructions() {
            return "Please set the hour...";
        }

        public int getSelectedValue() {
            return hour;
        }

    }



    public class MinuteSetupState implements ClockSetupState {

        private ClockSetup clockSetup;
        private int minute;

        public MinuteSetupState(ClockSetup clockSetup) {
            this.clockSetup = clockSetup;
            minute = Calendar.getInstance().get(Calendar.MINUTE);
        }
```

```
public void previousValue() {
    if (minute > 0) {
        minute--;
    }
}

public void nextValue() {
    if (minute < 59) {
        minute++;
    }
}

public void selectValue() {
    System.out.println("Minute set to " + minute);
    clockSetup.setState
            (clockSetup.getFinishedSetupState());
}

public String getInstructions() {
    return "Please set the minute...";
}

public int getSelectedValue() {
    return minute;
}

}
```

This just leaves the `FinishedSetupState` class which doesn't need to transition to a different state:

```
public class FinishedSetupState implements ClockSetupState {

    private ClockSetup clockSetup;

    public FinishedSetupState(ClockSetup clockSetup) {
        this.clockSetup = clockSetup;
    }

    public void previousValue() {
        System.out.println("Ignored...");
    }

    public void nextValue() {
        System.out.println("Ignored...");
    }

    public void selectValue() {
        Calendar selectedDate = clockSetup.getSelectedDate();
        System.out.println("Date set to: " + selectedDate.getTime());
    }

    public String getInstructions() {
        return "Press knob to view selected date...";
```

```
        }

    public int getSelectedValue() {
        throw new UnsupportedOperationException
                            ("Clock setup finished");
    }

}
```

As mentioned, the 'context' class is `ClockSetup`, which holds references to each state and forwards to whichever is the current state:

```java
public class ClockSetup {

    // The various states the setup can be in...
    private ClockSetupState yearState;
    private ClockSetupState monthState;
    private ClockSetupState dayState;
    private ClockSetupState hourState;
    private ClockSetupState minuteState;
    private ClockSetupState finishedState;

    // The current state we are in...
    private ClockSetupState currentState;

    public ClockSetup() {
        yearState = new YearSetupState(this);
        monthState = new MonthSetupState(this);
        dayState = new DaySetupState(this);
        hourState = new HourSetupState(this);
        minuteState = new MinuteSetupState(this);
        finishedState = new FinishedSetupState(this);

        // Initial state is to set the year
        setState(yearState);
    }

    public void setState(ClockSetupState state) {
        currentState = state;
        System.out.println(currentState.getInstructions());
    }

    public void rotateKnobLeft() {
        currentState.previousValue();
    }

    public void rotateKnobRight() {
        currentState.nextValue();
    }

    public void pushKnob() {
        currentState.selectValue();
    }
```

```
    public ClockSetupState getYearSetupState() {
        return yearState;
    }

    public ClockSetupState getMonthSetupState() {
        return monthState;
    }

    public ClockSetupState getDaySetupState() {
        return dayState;
    }

    public ClockSetupState getHourSetupState() {
        return hourState;
    }

    public ClockSetupState getMinuteSetupState() {
        return minuteState;
    }

    public ClockSetupState getFinishedSetupState() {
        return finishedState;
    }

    public Calendar getSelectedDate() {
        return new GregorianCalendar(
                        yearState.getSelectedValue(),
                        monthState.getSelectedValue(),
                        dayState.getSelectedValue(),
                        hourState.getSelectedValue(),
                        minuteState.getSelectedValue());
    }

}
```

We can simulate a user's example actions like this:

```
ClockSetup clockSetup = new ClockSetup();

// Setup starts in 'year' state
clockSetup.rotateKnobRight();
clockSetup.pushKnob(); // 1 year on

// Setup should now be in 'month' state
clockSetup.rotateKnobRight();
clockSetup.rotateKnobRight();
clockSetup.pushKnob(); // 2 months on

// Setup should now be in 'day' state
clockSetup.rotateKnobRight();
clockSetup.rotateKnobRight();
clockSetup.rotateKnobRight();
clockSetup.pushKnob(); // 3 days on
```

```
// Setup should now be in 'hour' state
clockSetup.rotateKnobLeft();
clockSetup.rotateKnobLeft();
clockSetup.pushKnob(); // 2 hours back

// Setup should now be in 'minute' state
clockSetup.rotateKnobRight();
clockSetup.pushKnob(); // 1 minute on

// Setup should now be in 'finished' state
clockSetup.pushKnob(); // to display selected date
```

Running the above should result in the following output relative to your current system date and time, with the above adjustments made.

```
Please set the year...
Year set to 2013
Please set the month...
Month set to 10
Please set the day...
Day set to 25
Please set the hour...
Hour set to 0
Please set the minute...
Minute set to 4
Press knob to view selected date...
Date set to: Mon Nov 25 04:17:00 GMT 2013
```

22. Strategy

Type	Behavioural
Purpose	Define a family of algorithms, encapsulate each one, and make them interchangeable. *Strategy* lets the algorithm vary independently from clients that use it.

The Foobar Motor Company wishes to implement a new type of automatic gearbox for their cars that will be able to be switched between its standard mode and a special 'sport' mode. The different modes will base the decision of which gear should be selected depending upon the speed of travel, size of the engine and whether it is turbocharged. And it's quite possible they will want other modes in the future, such as for off-road driving.

Just as with the discussion in the chapter for the *State* pattern, it would be inflexible to use a series of if...else... statements to control the different gearbox modes directly inside our vehicle classes. Instead, we shall encapsulate the concept that varies and define a separate hierarchy so that each different gearbox mode is a separate class, each in effect being a different 'strategy' that gets applied. This approach allows the actual strategy being used to be isolated from the vehicle. In our example, we shall only apply this to the cars:

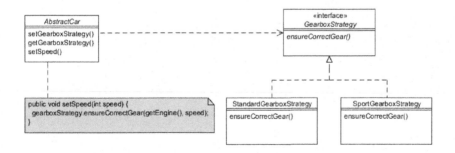

Figure 22.1 : Strategy pattern

The `GearboxStrategy` interface defines the method to control the gear:

```
public interface GearboxStrategy {

    public void ensureCorrectGear(Engine engine, int speed);

}
```

There are two implementing classes; `StandardGearboxStrategy` and `SportGearboxStrategy`:

```
public class StandardGearboxStrategy implements GearboxStrategy {

    public void ensureCorrectGear(Engine engine, int speed) {
        int engineSize = engine.getSize();
        boolean turbo = engine.isTurbo();

        //  Some complicated code to determine correct gear
        //  setting based on engineSize, turbo & speed, etc.
        //  ... omitted ...

        System.out.println("Working out correct gear at " +
                        speed + "mph for a STANDARD gearbox");
    }

}
```

```
public class SportGearboxStrategy implements GearboxStrategy {

    public void ensureCorrectGear(Engine engine, int speed) {
        int engineSize = engine.getSize();
        boolean turbo = engine.isTurbo();

        //  Some complicated code to determine correct gear
        //  setting based on engineSize, turbo & speed, etc.
        //  ... omitted ...

        System.out.println("Working out correct gear at " +
                        speed + "mph for a SPORT gearbox");
    }

}
```

Our `AbstractCar` class is defined to hold a reference to the interface type (i.e. `GearboxStrategy`) and provide accessor methods so different strategies can be switched. There is also a setSpeed() method that delegates to whatever strategy is in effect. The pertinent code is marked in bold:

```
public abstract class AbstractCar extends AbstractVehicle {

    private GearboxStrategy gearboxStrategy;

    public AbstractCar(Engine engine) {
        this(engine, Vehicle.Colour.UNPAINTED);
    }

    public AbstractCar(Engine engine) {
        super(engine);

        //  Starts in standard gearbox mode (more economical)
        gearboxStrategy = new StandardGearboxStrategy();
    }

    // Allow the gearbox strategy to be changed...
    public void setGearboxStrategy(GearboxStrategy gs) {
        gearboxStrategy = gs;
    }

    public GearboxStrategy getGearboxStrategy() {
        return getGearboxStrategy();
    }

    public void setSpeed(int speed) {
        // Delegate to strategy in effect...
        gearboxStrategy.ensureCorrectGear(getEngine(), speed);
    }

}
```

Client programs just set the required strategy:

```
AbstractCar myCar = new Sport(new StandardEngine(2000));
myCar.setSpeed(20);
myCar.setSpeed(40);

System.out.println("Switching on sports mode gearbox...");
myCar.setGearboxStrategy(new SportGearboxStrategy());
myCar.setSpeed(20);
myCar.setSpeed(40);
```

This should result in the following output:

```
Working out correct gear at 20mph for a STANDARD gearbox
Working out correct gear at 40mph for a STANDARD gearbox
```

```
Switching on sports mode gearbox...
Working out correct gear at 20mph for a SPORT gearbox
Working out correct gear at 40mph for a SPORT gearbox
```

23. Template Method

Type	Behavioural
Purpose	Define the skeleton of an algorithm in a method, deferring some steps to subclasses. *Template Method* lets subclasses redefine certain steps of an algorithm without changing the algorithm's structure.

Each vehicle made by the Foobar Motor Company needs a small number of printed booklets to be produced and provided to the buyer, such as an Owner's Manual and a Service History booklet. The way booklets are produced always follows the same set of steps, but each different type of booklet might need to do each of the individual steps in a slightly different way.

The *Template Method* pattern enables the definition of one or more abstract methods that are called through a 'template method'. The simple hierarchy is as follows:

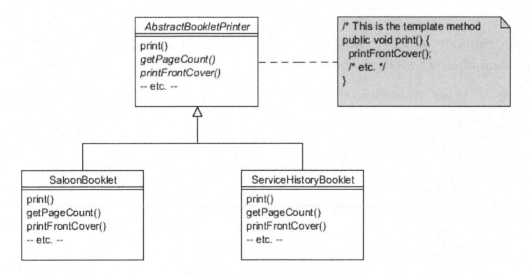

Figure 23.1 : Template Method pattern

The `AbstractBookletPrinter` **class defines several** `protected abstract` **methods and one** `public final` 'template method' **that makes use of the** **abstract methods (the method is made** `final` **to prevent it from being** **overridden):**

```
public abstract class AbstractBookletPrinter {

    protected abstract int getPageCount();
    protected abstract void printFrontCover();
    protected abstract void printTableOfContents();
    protected abstract void printPage(int pageNumber);
    protected abstract void printIndex();
    protected abstract void printBackCover();

    // This is the 'template method'
    public final void print() {
        printFrontCover();
        printTableOfContents();
        for (int i = 1; i <= getPageCount(); i++) {
            printPage(i);
        }
        printIndex();
        printBackCover();
    }

}
```

Each concrete subclass now only needs to provide the implementing code **for each abstract method, for example the** `SaloonBooklet` **class below:**

```
public class SaloonBooklet extends AbstractBookletPrinter {

    protected int getPageCount() {
        return 100;
    }

    protected void printFrontCover() {
        System.out.println
            ("Printing front cover for Saloon car booklet");
    }

    protected void printTableOfContents() {
        System.out.println
            ("Printing table of contents for Saloon car booklet");
    }

    protected void printPage(int pageNumber) {
        System.out.println
            ("Printing page " + pageNumber + " for Saloon car
```

```
                        booklet");
    }

    protected void printIndex() {
        System.out.println
            ("Printing index for Saloon car booklet");
    }

    protected void printBackCover() {
        System.out.println
            ("Printing back cover for Saloon car booklet");
    }

}
```

The `ServiceHistoryBooklet` **is very similar:**

```
public class ServiceHistoryBooklet extends AbstractBookletPrinter {

    protected int getPageCount() {
        return 12;
    }

    protected void printFrontCover() {
        System.out.println
            ("Printing front cover for service history booklet");
    }

    protected void printTableOfContents() {
        System.out.println
            ("Printing table of contents for service history
                booklet");
    }

    protected void printPage(int pageNumber) {
        System.out.println
            ("Printing page " + pageNumber + " for service history
                booklet");
    }

    protected void printIndex() {
        System.out.println
            ("Printing index for service history booklet");
    }

    protected void printBackCover() {
        System.out.println
            ("Printing back cover for service history booklet");
    }

}
```

While it is not essential from the point of view of the pattern for the abstract methods to be `protected`, it is often the case that this is the most appropriate access level to assign since they are only intended for overriding and not for direct invocation by client objects.

Also note that it's perfectly acceptable for some of the methods called from the 'template method' to not be abstract but have a default implementation provided. But when at least one abstract method is being called, it qualifies as the *Template Method* pattern.

Client programs merely need to instantiate the required concrete class and invoke the `print()` method:

```
System.out.println("About to print a booklet for Saloon cars");
AbstractBookletPrinter saloonBooklet = new SaloonBooklet();
saloonBooklet.print();

System.out.println("About to print a service history booklet");
AbstractBookletPrinter serviceBooklet = new ServiceHistoryBooklet();
serviceBooklet.print();
```

24. Visitor

Type	Behavioural
Purpose	Represent a method to be performed on the elements of an object structure. *Visitor* lets you define a new method without changing the classes of the elements on which it operates.

Sometimes a class hierarchy and its code become substantive, and yet it is known that future requirements will be inevitable. An example for the Foobar Motor Company is the `Engine` hierarchy which looks like this:

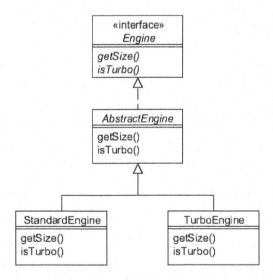

Figure 24.1 : Engine class hierarchy

In reality, the code within the `AbstractEngine` class is likely to be composed of a multitude of individual components, such as a camshaft, piston, some spark plugs, etc. If we need to add some functionality that traverses these components then the natural way is to just add a method to `AbstractEngine`. But maybe we know there are potentially many such new requirements and we would rather not have to keep adding methods directly into the hierarchy?

The *Visitor* pattern enables us to define just one additional method to add into the class hierarchy in such a way that lots of different types of new functionality can be added without any further changes. This is accomplished by means of a technique known as "double-despatch", whereby the invoked method issues a call-back to the invoking object.

The technique requires first the definition of an interface we shall call `EngineVisitor`:

```
public interface EngineVisitor {

    public void visit(Camshaft camshaft);
    public void visit(Engine engine);
    public void visit(Piston piston);
    public void visit(SparkPlug sparkPlug);

}
```

We will also define an interface called `Visitable` with an `acceptEngineVisitor()` method:

```
public interface Visitable {

    public void acceptEngineVisitor(EngineVisitor visitor);

}
```

The `Engine` interface you have met in previous chapters (although we will modify it slightly for this chapter). The `Camshaft`, `Piston` and `SparkPlug` classes are each very simple, as follows:

```
public class Camshaft implements Visitable {

    public void acceptEngineVisitor(EngineVisitor visitor) {
        visitor.visit(this);
    }

}


public class Piston implements Visitable {
```

```
    public void acceptEngineVisitor(EngineVisitor visitor) {
        visitor.visit(this);
    }

}


public class SparkPlug implements Visitable {

    public void acceptEngineVisitor(EngineVisitor visitor) {
        visitor.visit(this);
    }

}
```

As you can see, each of these classes defines a method called acceptEngineVisitor() that takes a reference to an EngineVisitor object as its argument. All the method does is invoke the visit() method of the passed-in EngineVisitor, passing back the object instance.

Our modified Engine interface also now defines the acceptEngineVisitor() method:

```
public interface Engine extends Visitable {

    public int getSize();
    public boolean isTurbo();

    public void acceptEngineVisitor(EngineVisitor visitor);

}
```

The AbstractEngine class therefore needs to implement this new method, which in this case traverses the individual components (camshaft, piston, spark plugs) invoking acceptEngineVisitor() on each:

```
public abstract class AbstractEngine implements Engine {

    private int size;
    private boolean turbo;

    private Camshaft camshaft;
    private Piston piston;
    private SparkPlug[] sparkPlugs;

    public AbstractEngine(int size, boolean turbo) {
```

```
        this.size = size;
        this.turbo = turbo;

        // Create a camshaft, piston and 4 spark plugs...`
        camshaft = new Camshaft();
        piston = new Piston();
        sparkPlugs = new SparkPlug[]{new SparkPlug(),
                                     new SparkPlug(),
                                     new SparkPlug(),
                                     new SparkPlug()};
    }

    public int getSize() {
        return size;
    }

    public boolean isTurbo() {
        return turbo;
    }

    public void acceptEngineVisitor(EngineVisitor visitor) {
        // Visit each component first...
        camshaft.acceptEngineVisitor(visitor);
        piston.acceptEngineVisitor(visitor);
        for (SparkPlug eachSparkPlug : sparkPlugs) {
            eachSparkPlug.acceptEngineVisitor(visitor);
        }

        // Now visit the receiver...
        visitor.visit(this);
    }

    public String toString() {
        return getClass().getSimpleName() +
                " (" + size + ")");
    }

}
```

Now we shall create an actual implementation of `EngineVisitor` so you can see how we can easily add additional functionality to engines without any further changes to any engine hierarchy class. The first thing we shall do is to define some clever electronic gizmo that can be attached to an engine that will automatically check each component and diagnose any faults. We therefore define the `EngineDiagnostics` class:

```
public class EngineDiagnostics implements EngineVisitor {

    public void visit(Camshaft camshaft) {
        System.out.println("Diagnosing the camshaft");
    }
```

```
public void visit(Engine engine) {
    System.out.println("Diagnosing the unit engine");
}

public void visit(Piston piston) {
    System.out.println("Diagnosing the piston");
}

public void visit(SparkPlug sparkPlug) {
    System.out.println("Diagnosing a single spark plug");
}

}
```

We also want to print an inventory of how many of each type of component there is within an engine, so we also have an EngineInventory class:

```
public class EngineInventory implements EngineVisitor {

    private int camshaftCount;
    private int pistonCount;
    private int sparkPlugCount;

    public EngineInventory() {
        camshaftCount = 0;
        pistonCount = 0;
        sparkPlugCount = 0;
    }

    public void visit(Camshaft p) {
        camshaftCount++;
    }

    public void visit(Engine e) {
        System.out.println("The engine has: " +
                           camshaftCount + " camshaft(s), " +
                           pistonCount + " piston(s), and " +
                           sparkPlugCount + " spark plug(s)");
    }

    public void visit(Piston p) {
        pistonCount++;
    }

    public void visit(SparkPlug sp) {
        sparkPlugCount++;
    }

}
```

The following diagram summarises how all of these classes interact:

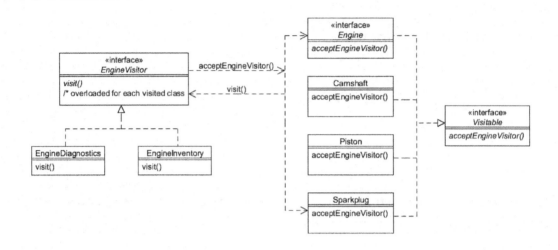

Figure 24.2 : Visitor pattern

Client programs now only need to invoke the `acceptEngineVisitor()` method on an instance of `Engine`, passing in the appropriate `EngineVisitor` object:

```
// Create an engine...
Engine engine = new StandardEngine(1300);

// Run diagnostics on the engine...
engine.acceptEngineVisitor(new EngineDiagnostics());
```

The above will result in the following output:

```
Diagnosing the camshaft
Diagnosing the piston
Diagnosing a single spark plug
Diagnosing a single spark plug
Diagnosing a single spark plug
Diagnosing a single spark plug
Diagnosing the unit engine
```

And to obtain the inventory (using the same `Engine` instance):

```
// Run inventory on the engine...
engine.acceptEngineVisitor(new EngineInventory());
```

The output should show:

```
The engine has: 1 camshaft(s), 1 piston(s), and 4 spark plug(s)
```

Part V. Other Useful Patterns

This part describes four additional patterns you should find useful in practical applications.

- *Null Object*: Define a class that enables the processing of `null` values;

- *Simple Factory*: Delegate the instantiation of objects;

- *Model View Controller*: Separate a user interface component's screen representation from its underlying data and functionality;

- *Layers*: Partition an application into separate modular levels that communicate hierarchically.

25. Null Object

As any Java programmer soon discovers, software testing often throws up NullPointerException messages. Sometimes, the only way around this is to specifically test for null before performing an operation, which puts an extra onus on the programmer.

Suppose a vehicle's instrument panel contains three slots for warning lights (such as for low oil level or low brake fluid level). A particular vehicle might only use these two lights, with the third slot empty, represented by null within Java. Looping through the slots would require a specific test to prevent a NullPointerException being thrown:

```
//  OilLevelLight &  BrakeFluidLight are each types of WarningLight
WarningLight[] lights = new WarningLight[3];
lights[0] = new OilLevelLight();
lights[1] = new BrakeFluidLight();
lights[2] = null; //  empty slot

for (WarningLight currentLight : lights) {
    if (currentLight != null) {
        currentLight.turnOn();
        currentLight.turnOff();
        System.out.println(currentLight.isOn());
    }
}
```

An approach that can help prevent the need to test for null is to create a 'null object' class as part of the class hierarchy. This class will implement the same interface but perform no actual function, as illustrated in the following figure:

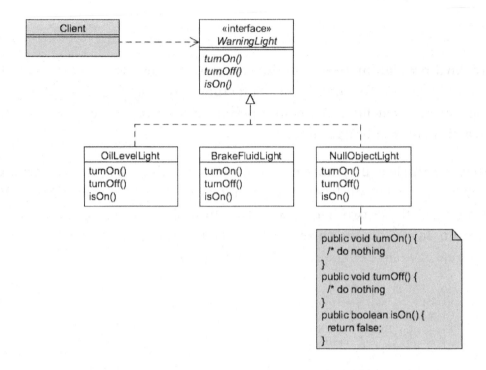

Figure 25.1 : Null Object pattern

The `WarningLight` interface defines the methods `turnOn()`, `turnOff()` and `isOn()`:

```
public interface WarningLight {

    public void turnOn();
    public void turnOff();
    public boolean isOn();
}
```

The `OilLightLevel` and `BrakeFluidLevel` classes each implement the `WarningLight` interface and provide the appropriate code to switch the light on or off:

```
public class OilLevelLight implements WarningLight {

    private boolean on;
```

```
    public void turnOn() {
        on = true;
        System.out.println("Oil level light ON");
    }

    public void turnOff() {
        on = false;
        System.out.println("Oil level light OFF");
    }

    public boolean isOn() {
        return on;
    }
}


public class BrakeFluidLight implements WarningLight {

    private boolean on;

    public void turnOn() {
        on = true;
        System.out.println("Brake fluid light ON");
    }

    public void turnOff() {
        on = false;
        System.out.println("Brake fluid light OFF");
    }

    public boolean isOn() {
        return on;
    }
}
```

For the *Null Object* pattern we also create a `NullObjectLight` class that implements the `WarningLight` interface but performs no actual processing:

```
public class NullObjectLight implements WarningLight {

    public void turnOn() {
        // Do nothing...
    }

    public void turnOff() {
        // Do nothing...
    }

    public boolean isOn() {
        return false;
    }
}
```

```
}
```

Now our client code can be simplified since we no longer need to test if a slot is `null`, provided we make use of the null object:

```java
WarningLight[] lights = new WarningLight[3];
lights[0] = new OilLevelLight();
lights[1] = new BrakeFluidLight();
lights[2] = new NullObjectLight(); // empty slot

// No need to test for null...
for (WarningLight currentLight : lights) {
    currentLight.turnOn();
    currentLight.turnOff();
    System.out.println(currentLight.isOn());
}
```

Note that for *Null Object* getter methods you will need to return whatever seems sensible as a default; hence above the `isOn()` method returns `false` since it represents a non-existent light.

26. Simple Factory

In the main section of this book we looked at both the *Factory Method* pattern and the *Abstract Factory* pattern. The *Simple Factory* pattern[1] is a commonly used simplified means of delegating the instantiation of objects to a specific class (the 'factory').

We shall assume here that the Foobar Motor Company manufactures two types of gearbox; an automatic gearbox and a manual gearbox. Client programs might need to create one or the other based upon a condition, as illustrated by the following code fragment (assuming the classes are defined within a class hierarchy):

```
Gearbox selectedGearbox = null;
if (typeWanted = "automatic") {
    selectedGearbox = new AutomaticGearbox();
} else if (typeWanted = "manual") {
    selectedGearbox = new ManualGearbox();
}

// Do something with selectedGearbox...
```

While the above code will of course work, what happens if more than one client program needs to perform a similar selection? We would have to repeat the if...else... statements in each client program, and if a new type of gearbox is subsequently manufactured we would have to track down every place the if...else... block is used.

Remembering the principle of encapsulating the concept that varies, we can instead delegate the selection and instantiation process to a specific class, known as the 'factory', just for that purpose. Client programs then only make use of the create() method of the factory, as illustrated in the diagram below:

---

[1]Some authors state that *Simple Factory* is more of an object-oriented programming idiom rather than a full-fledged pattern.

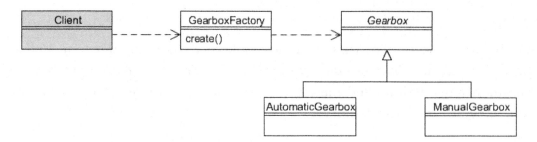

Figure 26.1 : Simple Factory pattern

The abstract `Gearbox` class in our simple example merely defines a no-argument constructor:

```
public abstract class Gearbox {

    public Gearbox() {}

}
```

The `AutomaticGearbox` and `ManualGearbox` classes each extend `Gearbox` for their respective types:

```
public class AutomaticGearbox extends Gearbox {

    public AutomaticGearbox() {
        System.out.println("New automatic gearbox created");
    }

}
```

```
public class ManualGearbox extends Gearbox {

    public ManualGearbox() {
        System.out.println("New manual gearbox created");
    }

}
```

We now need to create our `GearboxFactory` class that is capable of instantiating the appropriate `Gearbox`:

```
public class GearboxFactory {

    public enum Type {AUTOMATIC, MANUAL};

    public static Gearbox create(Type type) {
        if (type == Type.AUTOMATIC) {
            return new AutomaticGearbox();

        } else {
            return new ManualGearbox();
        }
    }

}
```

The `create()` method takes care of the selection and instantiation, and thus isolates each client program from repeating code. We have made the method `static` purely for convenience; it is not a requirement of the pattern.

Client programs now obtain the type of gearbox by means of the factory:

```
// Create an automatic gearbox
Gearbox auto = GearboxFactory.create(GearboxFactory.Type.AUTOMATIC);

// Create a manual gearbox
Gearbox manual = GearboxFactory.create(GearboxFactory.Type.MANUAL);
```

27. Model View Controller

The Foobar Motor Company's satellite-navigation system includes a visual display of the current location, the direction of travel and an indication of the current speed. There is also an input device; controls where you set the destination, etc. A fully fledged simulation is far beyond the scope of this book, so instead we will use a very simplified interface that merely lets you set the direction of travel (North, South, West and East) and the current speed (up to 30mph), without regard to any roads, etc..

The user interface will look like this:

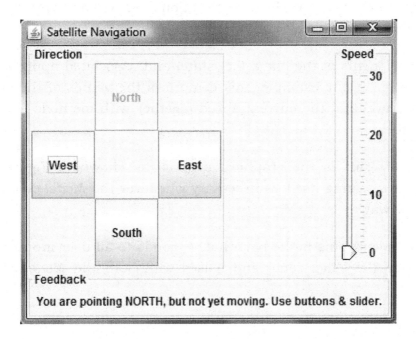

Figure 27.1 : Satellite navigation user interface

As you can see from the above, there are buttons to change direction and a slider to adjust the speed. The 'Feedback' section at the bottom of the screen automatically adjusts itself to your selections[1]. Note that each time

---

[1]You can download an executable JAR of this program from the book's website.

you click one of the direction buttons that button is disabled, and the previously selected button is re-enabled. The program initially starts by pointing North but with a speed of zero.

This is a straightforward program that would be entirely possible to code within a single class. But as graphical applications become more complex, it greatly simplifies development and maintenance if you separate the major parts of the program.

The *Model View Controller* pattern (often abbreviated to MVC) is a way of achieving a looser coupling between the constituent parts, and is a tried-and-tested approach to graphical applications. There are typically three parts at play in GUI applications:

1. *The "Model"*. This is the 'data' (i.e. state) and associated application or 'business' logic. In our example, this comprises the values of the current direction of travel and the current speed together with methods to update and return them.

2. *The "View"*. This is the graphical display, as shown in Figure 27.1, automatically updating itself as necessary whenever the *Model* changes its state in some way.

3. *The "Controller"*. This is the part that responds to all user input (button clicks, moving the slider, etc.) and liaises with both the *Model* and the *View*.

Each of the above three parts will be in a separate class, which can be visualised as follows:

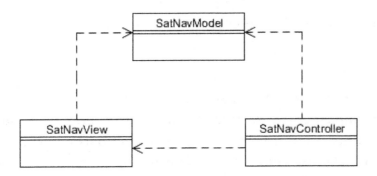

Figure 27.2 : Model View Controller pattern

These classes interrelate in the following way:

- `SatNavModel` contains methods to set and get both the direction and speed. It is 'observable'[1] and will notify interested observers whenever either the direction or the speed has changed, but has no direct knowledge of any other class;

- `SatNavView` defines the graphical frame and user-interface display. It holds a reference to `SatNavModel` so it can listen to state changes in the *Model* and query its state as needed to keep the display up-to-date automatically;

- `SatNavController` holds a reference to both `SatNavModel` and `SatNavView`. It handles button clicks and movement of the speed slider, updating the *Model* and liaising with the *View* as needed.

Just as with the other patterns described in this book, there are variations in how MVC can be structured, and the above might be described as the 'classical' approach. Java components (including the Swing components)

---

[1]See the *Observer* pattern

often use a modified version of MVC in which the View and Controller are combined into a single class, but for the purposes of this book we will use the full three-class separation to present the pattern.

We shall start with the *Model*, which in our case is the class SatNavModel. This has been implemented so that it could easily become a JavaBean, although that is not a requirement of MVC. The important point is that it has direct knowledge of neither the *View* nor the *Controller*, and could therefore be plugged into all sorts of other applications without any changes being required.

```java
public class SatNavModel implements Serializable {

    // Used when notifying listeners so they know what has changed
    public static final String DIRECTION_CHANGE = "direction";
    public static final String SPEED_CHANGE = "speed";

    // The directions we can travel
    public enum Direction {NORTH, SOUTH, EAST, WEST};

    // The current direction and speed
    private Direction currentDirection;
    private int currentSpeed;

    // This class is observable
    private PropertyChangeSupport changeSupport;


    public SatNavModel() {
        currentDirection = Direction.NORTH;
        currentSpeed = 0;
        changeSupport = new PropertyChangeSupport(this);
    }

    public void setDirection(Direction newDirection) {
        if (newDirection != currentDirection) {
            Direction previousDirection = currentDirection;
            currentDirection = newDirection;
            changeSupport.firePropertyChange
                                  (DIRECTION_CHANGE,
                                   previousDirection,
                                   currentDirection);

        }
    }

    public Direction getDirection() {
        return currentDirection;
    }
```

```
public void setSpeed(int newSpeed) {
    if (newSpeed != currentSpeed) {
        int previousSpeed = currentSpeed;
        currentSpeed = newSpeed;
        changeSupport.firePropertyChange
                            (SPEED_CHANGE,
                            previousSpeed,
                            currentSpeed);

    }
}

public int getSpeed() {
    return currentSpeed;
}

public void addPropertyChangeListener
        (PropertyChangeListener pcl) {
    changeSupport.addPropertyChangeListener(pcl);
}

public void removePropertyChangeListener
        (PropertyChangeListener pcl) {
    changeSupport.removePropertyChangeListener(pcl);
}

}
```

As you can see, the only link with other classes is through its observers (we are using the `PropertyChangeSupport` class in the `java.beans` package to facilitate this). Each time the direction or speed is modified its observers (also known as listeners) are notified.

The graphical display is performed by the `SatNavView` class using standard Swing components. It takes a reference to the `SatNavModel` in its constructor, to register itself as an observer of the model (so it needs to implement the `PropertyChangeListener` interface). Whenever it detects a model change the `propertyChange()` method is called, enabling the *View* to update its display accordingly. There are also methods to allow the UI controls to be observed (by, for example, the *Controller*).

```
public class SatNavView implements PropertyChangeListener {

    // The view needs a reference to the model
    private SatNavModel model;
```

```java
// The view uses a JFrame
private JFrame viewingFrame;

// UI controls to change direction and speed
private JButton northButton, southButton, westButton, eastButton;
private JSlider speedSlider;

// UI feedback to show current direction and speed
private String directionString, speedString;
private JLabel feedbackLabel;


public SatNavView(SatNavModel model) {
    this.model = model;

    // The view listens for changes to the model
    model.addPropertyChangeListener(this);

    // Initialise the UI
    viewingFrame = new JFrame("Satellite Navigation");
    viewingFrame.setDefaultCloseOperation
        (JFrame.EXIT_ON_CLOSE);

    northButton = new JButton("North");
    disableNorthButton(); // Default direction

    southButton = new JButton("South");
    westButton = new JButton("West");
    eastButton = new JButton("East");

    speedSlider = new JSlider(JSlider.VERTICAL, 0, 30, 0);
    speedSlider.setMajorTickSpacing(10);
    speedSlider.setMinorTickSpacing(1);
    speedSlider.setPaintTicks(true);
    speedSlider.setPaintLabels(true);

    directionString = "You are pointing " +
                            model.getDirection();
    speedString = "but not yet moving. Use buttons &
        slider.";
    feedbackLabel = new JLabel(directionString +
                                ", " +
                                speedString);

    // Layout the direction buttons
    JPanel directionPanel = new JPanel(new GridLayout(3, 3));
    directionPanel.setBorder(new TitledBorder("Direction"));
    directionPanel.add(new JLabel(""));
    directionPanel.add(northButton);
    directionPanel.add(new JLabel(""));
    directionPanel.add(westButton);
    directionPanel.add(new JLabel(""));
    directionPanel.add(eastButton);
    directionPanel.add(new JLabel(""));
    directionPanel.add(southButton);
    directionPanel.add(new JLabel(""));
```

```
        // Layout the slider
        JPanel speedPanel = new JPanel();
        speedPanel.setBorder(new TitledBorder("Speed"));
        speedPanel.add(speedSlider);

        // Layout the feedback
        JPanel feedbackPanel = new JPanel();
        feedbackPanel.setBorder(new TitledBorder("Feedback"));
        feedbackPanel.add(feedbackLabel);

        // Position the panels onto the frame
        JPanel framePanel = new JPanel(new BorderLayout());
        framePanel.add(directionPanel, BorderLayout.CENTER);
        framePanel.add(speedPanel, BorderLayout.EAST);
        framePanel.add(feedbackPanel, BorderLayout.SOUTH);

        viewingFrame.add(framePanel);
    }

    public void show() {
        // Show the view sized and centered
        viewingFrame.pack();
        viewingFrame.setLocationRelativeTo(null);
        viewingFrame.setVisible(true);
    }

    // The controller will register as a listener using these methods
    public void addNorthButtonListener(ActionListener al) {
        northButton.addActionListener(al);
    }

    public void addSouthButtonListener(ActionListener al) {
        southButton.addActionListener(al);
    }

    public void addWestButtonListener(ActionListener al) {
        westButton.addActionListener(al);
    }

    public void addEastButtonListener(ActionListener al) {
        eastButton.addActionListener(al);
    }

    public void addSliderListener(ChangeListener cl) {
        speedSlider.addChangeListener(cl);
    }

    // The controller will call these methods to enable UI controls
    public void enableNorthButton() {
        northButton.setEnabled(true);
    }

    public void disableNorthButton() {
        northButton.setEnabled(false);
    }
```

```java
public void enableSouthButton() {
    southButton.setEnabled(true);
}

public void disableSouthButton() {
    southButton.setEnabled(false);
}

public void enableWestButton() {
    westButton.setEnabled(true);
}

public void disableWestButton() {
    westButton.setEnabled(false);
}

public void enableEastButton() {
    eastButton.setEnabled(true);
}

public void disableEastButton() {
    eastButton.setEnabled(false);
}

// Called by the model when its state changes
public void propertyChange(PropertyChangeEvent pce) {
    if (model.getSpeed() == 0) {
        directionString = "You are pointing " +
                            model.getDirection();
        speedString = "but are not currently moving.";

    } else if (pce.getPropertyName().equals
        (SatNavModel.DIRECTION_CHANGE)) {
        SatNavModel.Direction newDirection =
                (SatNavModel.Direction) pce.getNewValue();
        directionString = "Now travelling " + newDirection;
        speedString = "travelling at " +
                                        model.getSpeed();

    } else if (pce.getPropertyName().equals
        (SatNavModel.SPEED_CHANGE)) {
        int oldSpeed = (Integer) pce.getOldValue();
        int newSpeed = (Integer) pce.getNewValue();
        if (oldSpeed < newSpeed) {
            speedString = "and you have sped up to " +
                                model.getSpeed();

        } else {
            speedString = "and you have slowed down to " +
                                model.getSpeed();
        }
    }

    feedbackLabel.setText(directionString +
                            ", " +
                            speedString);
}
```

```
}
```

The SatNavController class is responsible for handling the user input, which in this case can be either clicking one of the direction buttons or moving the speed slider. In response to the user input the *Model* state needs to be updated, and there is therefore a reference to both SatNavView and SatNavModel in the constructor. The class sets itself up to listen out for user input and reacts accordingly:

```
public class SatNavController {

    // Need a reference to both the model and the view
    private SatNavModel model;
    private SatNavView view;


    public SatNavController(SatNavModel model, SatNavView view) {
        this.model = model;
        this.view = view;

        // The controller needs to listen to the view
        view.addNorthButtonListener(new NorthButtonListener());
        view.addSouthButtonListener(new SouthButtonListener());
        view.addWestButtonListener(new WestButtonListener());
        view.addEastButtonListener(new EastButtonListener());
        view.addSliderListener(new SliderListener());
    }


    // Inner classes which serve as view listeners
    private class NorthButtonListener implements ActionListener {
        public void actionPerformed(ActionEvent event) {
            view.disableNorthButton();
            view.enableSouthButton();
            view.enableWestButton();
            view.enableEastButton();
            model.setDirection(SatNavModel.Direction.NORTH);
        }
    }

    private class SouthButtonListener implements ActionListener {
        public void actionPerformed(ActionEvent event) {
            view.enableNorthButton();
            view.disableSouthButton();
            view.enableWestButton();
            view.enableEastButton();
            model.setDirection(SatNavModel.Direction.SOUTH);
        }
    }
```

```
    private class WestButtonListener implements ActionListener {
        public void actionPerformed(ActionEvent event) {
            view.enableNorthButton();
            view.enableSouthButton();
            view.disableWestButton();
            view.enableEastButton();
            model.setDirection(SatNavModel.Direction.WEST);
        }
    }

    private class EastButtonListener implements ActionListener {
        public void actionPerformed(ActionEvent event) {
            view.enableNorthButton();
            view.enableSouthButton();
            view.enableWestButton();
            view.disableEastButton();
            model.setDirection(SatNavModel.Direction.EAST);
        }
    }

    private class SliderListener implements ChangeListener {
        public void stateChanged(ChangeEvent event) {
            JSlider slider = (JSlider) event.getSource();
            model.setSpeed(slider.getValue());
        }
    }

}
```

Running the application is now as simple as instantiating the above classes and invoking the show() command defined in the *View*:

```
// Create the MVC classes
SatNavModel model = new SatNavModel();
SatNavView view = new SatNavView(model);
SatNavController controller = new SatNavController(model, view);

// Show the view
view.show();
```

28. Layers

As applications grow larger they can become unwieldy to manage, with lots of interconnections leading to increased coupling. The *Layers* pattern addresses this by partitioning an application into two or more layers in a hierarchy, where each layer communicates only with the layer immediately below it. This approach helps to modularise applications and can help lower the coupling between classes.

Client-server (2-tier) architecture

A simple example of the *Layers* pattern would be the client-server model, where a "client" (such as a web browser) communicates with a "server" (such as a web server) in order to view a web page:

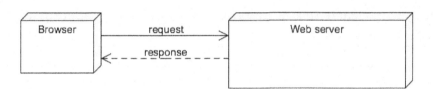

Figure 28.1 Client-server architecture

In Figure 28.1 you can see a browser sending a request to a web server which returns a response (such as a web page). If you imagine the client and server each being in their own package, then another way of viewing the above would be as follows:

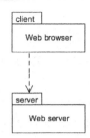

Figure 28.2 : Client-server package link

From Figure 28.2 you can infer that an object in the `client` package holds a reference to an object in the `server` package, such that the client can invoke a method on the server which may return a value in response.

> The client-server architecture is also known as a 2-tier architecture. The terms layer and tier are often used interchangeably, but "layer" more accurately refers to a logical partitioning and "tier" to a physical partitioning when each tier is potentially located on a different piece of hardware.

3-tier architecture

A common extension of the client-server architecture is where access to a data store is required, and therefore a third layer (or tier) is added to make a 3-tier architecture:

Figure 28.3 : 3-tier architecture

Figure 28.3 shows the browser sending a request to a server, and the server in turn sending a request to a database to obtain the requested information. This is then returned to the server which in turn returns it to the browser. Viewing the above as packages gives the following structure:

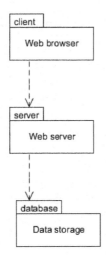

Figure 28.4 : 3-tier package links

From figure 28.4 you can infer that an object in the client package holds a reference to an object in the server package, just as in the 2-tier model. In addition, an object in the server package holds a reference to an object in the database package. However, the client has no direct access to the database – it has to communicate via the server layer in the middle.

> You are not limited to 3 tiers, of course. As applications grow in complexity additional layers may help to partition systems even further. This leads to the term *n-tier*, where *n* is the number of tiers.

Although the examples above have shown the common usages that typically utilise separate hardware, there is no reason why you cannot apply the structure of the *Layers* pattern in your own self-contained applications. Another pattern you have already seen which can usefully be used in conjunction with *Layers* is the *Façade* pattern, where each layer defines a facade object that the layer above communicates with. This approach can help hide the complexity of each layer behind the façade.

The next chapter provides a worked example that makes use of the *Layers* and *Façade* patterns, along with several other patterns that are commonly found in applications.

Part VI. Design Patterns in Practice

This part consists of a single chapter which shows a small, cut-down application that demonstrates example uses of certain common design patterns as described in this book. The patterns illustrated are:

- *Layers*

- *Singleton*

- *Façade*

- *Factory*

- *Observer*

- *Strategy*

- *Decorator*

29. Sample 3-Tier Application

This chapter develops a small, sample 3-tier[1] graphical application that makes use of a selection of commonly used design patterns. The application displays a list of engines that have come off the Foobar Motor Company production line (this means that the list may show the same engine type and size more than once), and provides facilities to build new engines and to save & restore the data to persistent storage. Please note that this is not intended to be production level software – the code has been greatly simplified in order to concentrate on the patterns involved.

The finished application will look as follows:

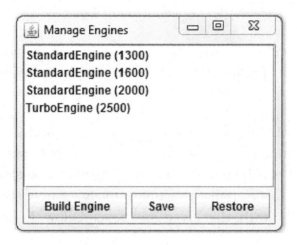

Figure 29.1 : Manage Engines frame

Each time the **Build Engine** button is clicked a dialogue will appear enabling you to create a new engine of your chosen type and size to be added to the list:

---

[1] The term "tier" is used loosely here since each tier is part of a single application on the same hardware. However, it could potentially be enhanced so that each tier exists on a separate system.

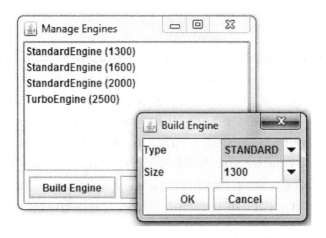

Figure 29.2 : Build Engine dialogue

The **Save** button will store the listed data to a file on your disk and the **Restore** button will replace the listed data with the values of the most recent save.

The application will be designed using a 3-tier architecture using the *Layers* pattern comprising a user interface layer, a business model layer, and a database layer. The classes for each layer will be stored in packages named `ui`, `business` and `db` respectively, such that each layer communicates only with the layer one level below it, as shown in the following figure:

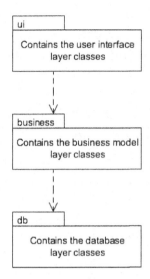

Figure 29.3 : 3-tier Layers pattern as packages

The database tier

Starting with the `db` package, we will refer to an object as an `Entity`. Since it is common for database tables to have a primary key we will define the class `EntityKeyGenerator` using the *Singleton* pattern `enum` technique as described in Chapter 6:

```
package db;

public enum EntityKeyGenerator {

    ENGINE;

    private int nextKey;

    synchronized int getNextKey() {
        return ++nextKey;
    }

}
```

To generate the next unique key for any `Engine` entity just needs a call to:

```
EntityKeyGenerator.ENGINE.getNextKey();
```

You could enhance the above to allow a separate series of numbers for vehicle entities just be defining an extra enum constant for VEHICLE inside EntityKeyGenerator above, but this is not needed for our simple example.

We will now define a simple EntityTable class that can store a Map of objects keyed by a sequential numeric id:

```java
package db;

import java.io.*;
import java.util.*;

public class EntityTable implements Serializable {

    private EntityKeyGenerator keyGenerator;
    private Map<Integer, Object> entities;
    private Collection<EntityListener> listeners;

    EntityTable(EntityKeyGenerator keyGenerator) {
        this.keyGenerator = keyGenerator;
        entities = new HashMap<Integer, Object>();
        listeners = new ArrayList<EntityListener>();
    }

    Object getByKey(Integer key) {
        return entities.get(key);
    }

    Collection<Object> getAll() {
        return entities.values();
    }

    Integer addEntity(Object value) {
        Integer key = keyGenerator.getNextKey();
        entities.put(key, value);
        fireEntityAdded(key, value);
        return key;
    }

    void restore(EntityTable restoredTable) {
        entities.clear();
        entities.putAll(restoredTable.entities);
        fireEntityRestored();
    }

    void addEntityListener(EntityListener listener) {
        listeners.add(listener);
    }

    void removeEntityListener(EntityListener listener) {
        listeners.remove(listener);
```

```
    }

    void fireEntityAdded(Integer key, Object value) {
        EntityEvent event = new EntityEvent(key, value);
        for (EntityListener listener : listeners) {
            listener.entityAdded(event);
        }
    }

    void fireEntityRestored() {
        EntityEvent event = new EntityEvent();
        for (EntityListener listener : listeners) {
            listener.entityRestored(event);
        }
    }

}
```

Note the following:

- The constructor requires an `EntityKeyGenerator` object which it can use to generate the next key for this particular entity type;

- The entities are stored in a `Map` keyed by an `Integer` (to represent the primary key) and where the value will be an `Object`. This allows the class to store any object type and therefore promotes loose-coupling;

- Methods are provided to return all entities or just one if the key is provided;

- The `addEntity()` method generates the next primary key which it returns, after adding the entity to the `Map`;

- The `restore()` method replaces the data with that provided in the argument;

- Methods are provided to add and remove `EntityListener` objects. This will enable other classes to be notified whenever a new entity is added to the database (or the data is restored), and is an example of the *Observer* pattern in action.

The `EntityEvent` class and `EntityListener` interface provide the notification mechanism as used by the `EntityTable` above.

The `EntityEvent` class stores a reference to the key and value of the entity object:

```
package db;

import java.util.*;

public class EntityEvent extends EventObject {

    private Object value;

    EntityEvent() {
        this(0, null); // used when restoring data
    }

    EntityEvent(Integer key, Object value) {
        super(key);
        this.value = value;
    }

    public Integer getKey() {
        return (Integer) getSource();
    }

    public Object getValue() {
        return value;
    }

}
```

The `EntityListener` interface declares methods indicating that a new entity was added to the database, or that the data was restored:

```
package db;

import java.util.*;

public interface EntityListener extends EventListener {

    public void entityAdded(EntityEvent event);
    public void entityRestored(EntityEvent event);

}
```

Saving the data to disk will be accomplished either by object serialization or by creating a CSV formatted text file. This suggests the *Strategy* pattern so that either approach can easily be switched in. The `AbstractEntityPersistenceStrategy` class provides the base class to define this:

```
package db;

import java.io.*;

public abstract class AbstractEntityPersistenceStrategy {

    String getFileName(EntityTable table) {
        return table.getClass().getSimpleName();
    }

    abstract String getFileSuffix();
    abstract void save(EntityTable table) throws IOException;
    abstract EntityTable restore(EntityTable table) throws
                                                    IOException;


}
```

The `EntitySerializationStrategy` class extends the above to implement the required methods:

```
package db;

import java.io.*;

public class EntitySerializationStrategy extends
                                AbstractEntityPersistenceStrategy {

    String getFileSuffix() {
        return ".ser";
    }

    void save(EntityTable table) throws IOException {
        File file = new File(getFileName(table) + getFileSuffix());
        FileOutputStream fos = new FileOutputStream(file);
        BufferedOutputStream bos = new BufferedOutputStream(fos);
        ObjectOutputStream oos = new ObjectOutputStream(bos);
        oos.writeObject(table);
        oos.close();
    }

    EntityTable restore(EntityTable table) throws IOException
    {
        File file = new File(getFileName(table) + getFileSuffix());
        FileInputStream fis = new FileInputStream(file);
        BufferedInputStream bis = new BufferedInputStream(fis);
```

```
            ObjectInputStream ois = new ObjectInputStream(bis);
            try {
                table = (EntityTable) ois.readObject();
            } catch (ClassNotFoundException ex) {
                throw new IOException(ex);
            }
            ois.close();
            return table;
        }

    }
```

Note in the save() and restore() methods the way InputStream and OutputStream objects are wrapped together. For example, inside save(), a FileOutputStream is wrapped inside a BufferedOutputStream which is in turn wrapped inside an ObjectOutputStream. This is an example of these Java supplied classes following the *Decorator* pattern, where each OutputStream object provides additional functionality.

The EntityCSVStrategy class likewise could be coded to use a CSV formatted file, although the code is omitted here:

```
package db;

import java.io.*;

public class EntityCSVStrategy extends
                            AbstractEntityPersistenceStrategy {

    String getFileSuffix() {
        return ".csv";
    }

    void save(EntityTable table) throws IOException {
        // code to save table data in CSV format (omitted)
    }

    EntityTable restore(EntityTable table) throws IOException {
        // code to restore table data from CSV format (omitted)
        return table;
    }

}
```

In order to simplify the job of any package that needs to make use of the database (which will be the `business` package in our case) there will be only a single point of access to all database functionality. This will provide a high-level view of the database which hides the internal structure and so also promotes loose-coupling. The *Façade* pattern used in conjunction with the *Singleton* pattern provides a means of defining a single point of access, as shown in the `DatabaseFacade` enum below:

```java
package db;

import java.io.*;

public enum DatabaseFacade {

    INSTANCE;

    private EntityTable engines;
    private AbstractEntityPersistenceStrategy persistenceStrategy;

    DatabaseFacade() {
        engines = new EntityTable(EntityKeyGenerator.ENGINE);

        // Set which persistence strategy to use
        // (maybe get from configuration settings somewhere)
        persistenceStrategy = new EntitySerializationStrategy();
    }

    public Object[] getAllEngines() {
        return engines.getAll().toArray();
    }

    public Object getEngine(Integer key) {
        return engines.getByKey(key);
    }

    public Integer addEngine(Object engine) {
        return engines.addEntity(engine);
    }

    public void addEngineListener(EntityListener listener) {
        engines.addEntityListener(listener);
    }

    public void removeEngineListener(EntityListener listener) {
        engines.removeEntityListener(listener);
    }

    public void saveEngines() throws IOException {
        persistenceStrategy.save(engines);
    }

    public void restoreEngines() throws IOException {
        EntityTable restoredEngines =
```

```
          persistenceStrategy.restore(engines);
   engines.restore(restoredEngines);
}

}
```

Note the following:

- The class is a *Singleton,* since the calling package should only use one *Façade* object;

- The class holds the `EntityTable` object to store the engines and methods to get all or one of them, as well as adding a new engine. If your system also managed vehicles then there would be equivalent variables and methods for this, too;

- The serialization persistence strategy is assumed, but you can see how easy it would be to use alternative strategies;

- Methods to add and remove listeners and to save and restore the data are delegated to the appropriate objects;

- You may have noticed that the constructor and methods within `EntityTable` and the persistence classes used package-private access. This is a means by which you can help enforce that external packages only go through the façade object methods, which are `public`.

The package diagram can now be shown with the classes of the db package included:

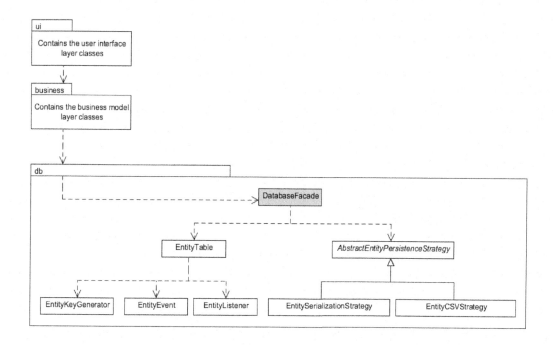

Figure 29.4 : Database package with Facade class

Note how the business tier communicates only through the DatabaseFaçade object. This has the effect of hiding the db package's complexity behind the façade.

The business tier

Moving on to the business package, this will consist primarily of the Engine hierarchy as used throughout this book:

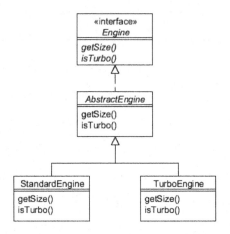

Figure 29.5 : Engine hierarchy

In order to facilitate `Engine` objects being serialised, its definition needs to be changed to extend the `Serializable` interface:

```
package business;

import java.io.*;

public interface Engine extends Serializable {

    public int getSize();
    public boolean isTurbo();

}
```

The other classes are unchanged, except that they of course now reside in a package called `business`.

Because there are two types of engine that can exist (standard and turbo), it will be useful to create a *Factory* class that creates objects of the correct type depending upon the supplied arguments. To this end, define a new class `EngineFactory` in the `business` package:

```
package business;
```

```
public class EngineFactory {

    public enum Type {STANDARD, TURBO};

    static Engine create(EngineFactory.Type type, int size) {
        if (type == Type.STANDARD) {
            return new StandardEngine(size);
        } else {
            return new TurboEngine(size);
        }
    }

    static Engine create(int size, boolean turbo) {
        return EngineFactory.create(turbo ?
                    Type.TURBO : Type.STANDARD, size);
    }

    private EngineFactory() {}

}
```

Note how the `create()` method is `static` and is overloaded so that client objects can either supply the enum `Type` value or a `boolean`.

Just as was done for the `db` package, the `business` package will have its own *façade* object, in this case the `BusinessFacade` singleton:

```
package business;

import db.*;
import java.io.*;

public enum BusinessFacade {

    INSTANCE;

    public Object[] getEngineTypes() {
        return EngineFactory.Type.values();
    }

    public Object[] getAllEngines() {
        return DatabaseFacade.INSTANCE.getAllEngines();
    }

    public Object addEngine(int size, Object type) {
        Engine engine = EngineFactory.create
                (size, type == EngineFactory.Type.TURBO);
        DatabaseFacade.INSTANCE.addEngine(engine);
        return engine;
```

```
    }

    public void saveEngines() throws IOException {
        DatabaseFacade.INSTANCE.saveEngines();
    }

    public void restoreEngines() throws IOException {
        DatabaseFacade.INSTANCE.restoreEngines();
    }

    public void addEngineListener(EntityListener listener) {
        DatabaseFacade.INSTANCE.addEngineListener(listener);
    }

    public void removeEngineListener(EntityListener listener) {
        DatabaseFacade.INSTANCE.removeEngineListener(listener);
    }

}
```

Note the following:

- The methods delegate to the appropriate `DatabaseFacade` methods;

- The `getEngineTypes()`, `getAllEngines()` and `addEngine()` methods have a return type of `Object` rather than of `Engine`. This means that the business package will be loosely-coupled with the ui package so that the latter does not depend upon the former's implementation details. The user interface can make use of the `toString()` method of the `Object` class to obtain the information to show in its list.

The package diagram can now be shown with the classes of the business package included:

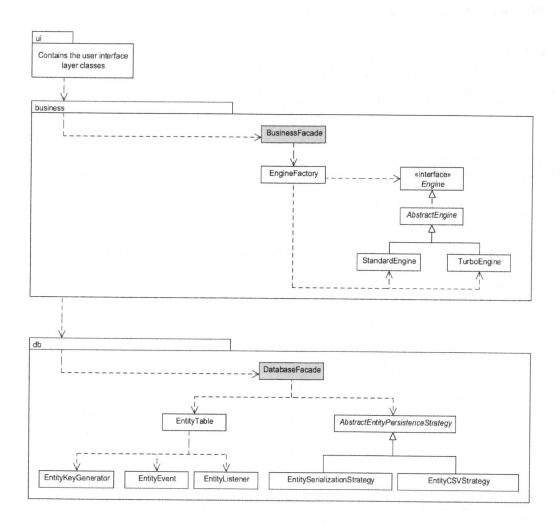

Figure 29.6 : Business package with Facade class

Note how the `ui` tier communicates only through the `BusinessFaçade` object. This has the effect of hiding the `business` package's complexity behind the façade.

The user interface tier

The ui package includes a ManageEnginesPanel class which shows a scrollable list of engines and some buttons:

```java
package ui;

import business.*;
import db.*;
import java.awt.*;
import java.awt.event.*;
import java.io.*;
import java.util.*;
import javax.swing.*;

public class ManageEnginesPanel extends JPanel
                                implements EntityListener {

    private Frame owner;
    private EngineListModel enginesModel;

    ManageEnginesPanel(final Frame owner) {
        super(new BorderLayout());
        this.owner = owner;

        // Scrollable list of engines
        enginesModel = new EngineListModel();
        add(new JScrollPane(new JList(enginesModel)),
                            BorderLayout.CENTER);

        // Buttons to add and save
        JPanel buttonPanel = new JPanel(new FlowLayout());

        JButton buildEngineButton =
                new JButton("Build Engine");
        buildEngineButton.addActionListener(new ActionListener() {
            public void actionPerformed(ActionEvent event) {
                new BuildEngineDialog(owner).show();
            }
        });
        buttonPanel.add(buildEngineButton);

        JButton saveButton = new JButton("Save");
        saveButton.addActionListener(new ActionListener() {
            public void actionPerformed(ActionEvent event) {
                try {
                    BusinessFacade.INSTANCE.saveEngines();
                } catch (IOException ex) {
                    JOptionPane.showMessageDialog
                            (ListEnginesPanel.this,
                             ex, "Error", JOptionPane.ERROR_MESSAGE);
                }
            }
        });
        buttonPanel.add(saveButton);
```

```java
        JButton restoreButton = new JButton("Restore");
        restoreButton.addActionListener(new ActionListener() {
            public void actionPerformed(ActionEvent event) {
                try {
                    BusinessFacade.INSTANCE.restoreEngines();
                } catch (IOException ex) {
                    JOptionPane.showMessageDialog
                            (ListEnginesPanel.this,
                             ex, "Error", JOptionPane.ERROR_MESSAGE);
                }
            }
        });
        buttonPanel.add(restoreButton);

        add(buttonPanel, BorderLayout.SOUTH);
    }

    public void entityAdded(EntityEvent event) {
        enginesModel.engineAdded(event.getValue());
    }

    public void entityRestored(EntityEvent event) {
        enginesModel.loadEngines();
    }


    // Inner class: ListModel for engines
    private class EngineListModel extends DefaultListModel {

        private java.util.List<Object> engines;

        EngineListModel() {
            engines = new ArrayList<Object>();
            loadEngines();
        }

        void loadEngines() {
            engines.clear();
            engines.addAll(
                        Arrays.asList(
                          BusinessFacade.INSTANCE.getAllEngines()
                        )
                      );
            fireContentsChanged(this, 0, engines.size() - 1);
        }

        public Object getElementAt(int index) {
            return engines.get(index);
        }

        public int getSize() {
            return engines.size();
        }

        void engineAdded(Object engine) {
            engines.add(engine);
```

```
                    fireContentsChanged(this, 0, engines.size() - 1);
            }

        }

    }
```

Note that the panel implements the `EntityListener` interface so that it gets notified whenever a new engine is added to the database, and so is making use of the *Observer* pattern.

The **Build Engine** button creates and displays a `BuildEngineDialog` object, which is as follows:

```
package ui;

import business.*;
import java.awt.*;
import java.awt.event.*;
import javax.swing.*;

public class BuildEngineDialog extends JDialog {

    private JComboBox typeCombo, sizeCombo;

    BuildEngineDialog(Frame owner) {
        super(owner, "Build Engine", true);
        setLayout(new BorderLayout());
        this.setLocationRelativeTo(owner);
        this.setDefaultCloseOperation(JDialog.DISPOSE_ON_CLOSE);

        // Form entry panel
        JPanel formPanel = new JPanel(new GridLayout(0, 2));

        typeCombo = new JComboBox
                (BusinessFacade.INSTANCE.getEngineTypes());
        formPanel.add(new JLabel("Type"));
        formPanel.add(typeCombo);

        sizeCombo = new JComboBox();
        sizeCombo.addItem(1300);
        sizeCombo.addItem(1600);
        sizeCombo.addItem(2000);
        sizeCombo.addItem(2500);
        formPanel.add(new JLabel("Size"));
        formPanel.add(sizeCombo);

        add(formPanel, BorderLayout.CENTER);

        // Buttons to submit or cancel
        JPanel buttonPanel = new JPanel(new FlowLayout());

        JButton okButton = new JButton("OK");
```

```
        okButton.addActionListener(new ActionListener() {
            public void actionPerformed(ActionEvent event) {
                BusinessFacade.INSTANCE.addEngine(
                        (Integer)sizeCombo.getSelectedItem(),
                        typeCombo.getSelectedItem());
                setVisible(false);
            }
        });
        buttonPanel.add(okButton);

        JButton cancelButton = new JButton("Cancel");
        cancelButton.addActionListener(new ActionListener() {
            public void actionPerformed(ActionEvent event) {
                setVisible(false);
            }
        });
        buttonPanel.add(cancelButton);

        add(buttonPanel, BorderLayout.SOUTH);
        pack();
    }
}
```

The **OK** button invokes the appropriate BusinessFacade method to add an engine with your selected criteria. On the main list panel the **Save** and **Restore** buttons also make appropriate calls to the BusinessFacade object methods so that the currently displayed data can be saved or restored.

The EnginesFrame class provides the frame that utilises ManageEnginesPanel:

```
package ui;

import business.*;
import java.awt.*;
import javax.swing.*;

public class EnginesFrame extends JFrame {

    private ManageEnginesPanel enginesPanel;

    public EnginesFrame () {
        super("Manage Engines");
        setDefaultCloseOperation(DISPOSE_ON_CLOSE);
        add(buildUI(), BorderLayout.CENTER);
        pack();
        setLocationRelativeTo(null);
    }

    private Component buildUI() {
```

```
        JPanel uiPanel = new JPanel(new BorderLayout());
        enginesPanel = new ManageEnginesPanel();
        BusinessFacade.INSTANCE.addEngineListener(enginesPanel);
        uiPanel.add(enginesPanel, BorderLayout.CENTER);
        return uiPanel;
    }

}
```

Finally, to invoke the frame you could create a fourth package called main
which contains a class called Main:

```
package main;

import ui.*;
import business.*;
import javax.swing.*;

public class Main {

    public static void main(String[] args) {
        // create some sample data
        BusinessFacade.INSTANCE.addEngine(1300,
                                EngineFactory.Type.STANDARD);
        BusinessFacade.INSTANCE.addEngine(1600,
                                EngineFactory.Type.STANDARD);
        BusinessFacade.INSTANCE.addEngine(2000,
                                EngineFactory.Type.STANDARD);
        BusinessFacade.INSTANCE.addEngine(2500,
                                EngineFactory.Type.TURBO);

        // start the ui
        SwingUtilities.invokeLater(new Runnable() {
            public void run() {
                new EnginesFrame().setVisible(true);
            }
        });
    }

}
```

The above class just creates some sample engines and starts the user
interface.

Part VII. Appendixes

This part contains the appendixes, which includes a brief explanation of the Unified Modeling Language (UML) diagram formats for those unfamiliar with UML, and a quick reference for each of the 23 main patterns.

Appendix A.   UML Diagrams

This book uses a simplified version of Unified Modeling Language (UML) diagrams to illustrate class hierarchies and usages for the patterns in this book. Each separate class is shown as a bounded rectangle with three horizontal sections, the top section containing the name of the class, the second section any relevant state (i.e. instance variables) and the third section containing the protocol (i.e. methods).

Representing types
Abstract classes, interfaces and abstract methods are shown in italicised text. The following figure shows an example of each sort of type and method:

Class
state
method1() method2()

AbstractClass
state
concreteMethod() *abstractMethod()*

«interface» *Interface*
method1() *method2()*

Figure A.1 : Normal class (left), abstract class (centre), interface (right)

The majority of diagrams in this book omit the state, thus leaving a small gap between the two horizontal bars (see the interface example in Figure A.1). This should not be taken to mean there is no state in the actual class; rather that it would have cluttered the diagram unnecessarily. Likewise, only relevant methods are listed, and not necessarily all. Unless specified otherwise, you can assume that all listed methods are `public`.

Representing inheritance

Inheritance is shown by a line connection between classes, with a hollow triangle pointing to the class being inherited or interfaces being implemented. Solid lines are shown for classes and dashed lines for interface connections:

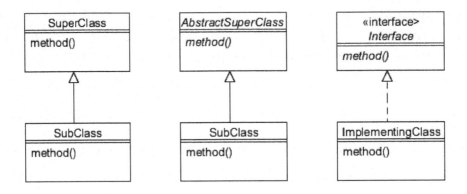

Figure A.2 : Extending a class (left & centre), implementing an interface (right)

Representing composition and usage

When one class 'uses' another (i.e. holds a reference to it), this is shown by a dashed line with an open arrow pointing toward the class being used. The usage is usually through passing a reference to the using object's constructor or a method, or by instantiating the object being used. In the following diagram each instance of ClassA holds or obtains a reference to an instance of ClassB:

Figure A.3 : ClassA uses ClassB

Code snippets

Where useful, snippets of code will be shown in a grey box attached to a class with a dashed line:

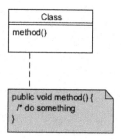

Figure A.4 : Code snippet

'Client' and other grey coloured classes

If a class rectangle is shown in grey this only for aesthetic purposes to separate it from other classes in the diagram. This is most often used in this book for 'client' classes, i.e. classes which make use of a particular pattern, as the following example for the *Chain of Responsibility* pattern illustrates:

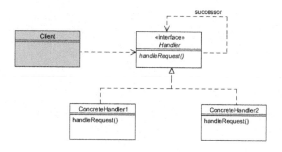

Figure A.5 : Client class in grey

Appendix B. Design Pattern Quick Reference

This appendix provides an alphabetical quick-reference of each of the 23 main design patterns described in this book in their most general form.

Note that many of the patterns make use of abstract classes or interfaces. In most cases these are interchangeable and the choice of which to use depends entirely upon your project requirements. It may also appear that the general form of a particular pattern described in this chapter differs from the detailed example in the main body of this book, but this is just a consequence of the fact that patterns are adaptable to the needs of the situation, and the general form should not be construed as the only or 'correct' approach.

Abstract Factory

Type	Creational
Purpose	Provide an interface for creating families of related or dependent objects without specifying their concrete classes.
Example usage	Commonly used when generating graphical 'widgets' for different look-and-feels. Used within the Java class libraries for that purpose.
Consequences	Isolates concrete classes. Enables easy exchange of product families. Promotes consistency among products.

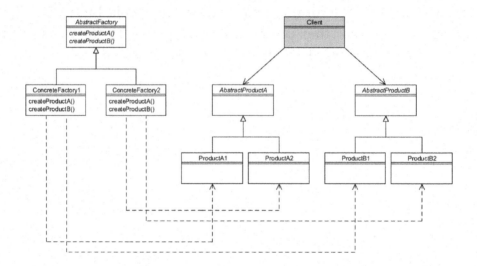

- `AbstractFactory` defines an interface for methods that create abstract product objects;

- `ConcreteFactory1` and `ConcreteFactory2` take care of instantiating the appropriate product families (e.g. `ConcreteFactory1` creates `ProductA1` and `ProductB1`);

- `AbstractProductA` and `AbstractProductB` defines the interface of each different type of product;

Client programs only use the interfaces declared by `AbstractFactory` and `AbstractProductA` and `AbstractProductB`.

Adapter

Type	Structural
Purpose	Convert the interface of a class into another interface clients expect. Adapter lets classes work together that couldn't otherwise because of incompatible interfaces.
Example usage	Integration of independent and incompatible classes. The Java class libraries define WindowAdapter as a convenience class that 'adapts' the WindowListener interface with default empty method implementations.
Consequences	A single adapter can work with many adaptees.

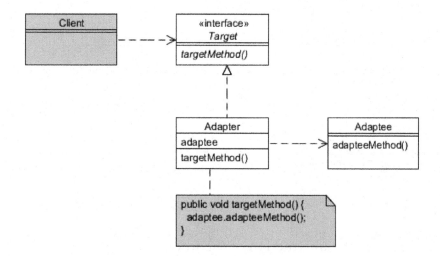

• Target refers to the interface that the client program requires;

• Adapter is the class used by client programs to forward requests to Adaptee;

• Adaptee is the class that needs adapting.

Bridge

Type	Structural
Purpose	Decouple an abstraction from its implementation so that each may vary independently.
Example usage	GUI frameworks and persistence frameworks.
Consequences	An implementation is not permanently bound to an interface, and can be switched at run-time.

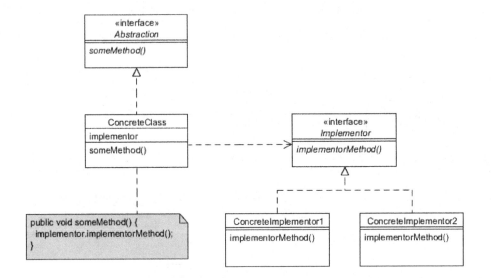

• Abstraction is the abstraction of the interface;

• ConcreteClass implements the Abstraction interface and holds a reference to Implementor. It provides an implementation in terms of Implementor;

• Implementor is the implementation interface which may be quite different to the Abstraction interface;

• ConcreteImplementor1 and ConcreteImplementor2 implement the Implementor interface.

Builder

Type	Creational
Purpose	Separate the construction of a complex object from its representation so that the same construction process can create different representations.
Example usage	Useful when there are several steps needed to create an object.
Consequences	Enables variations of a products internal representation. Isolates construction and representation.

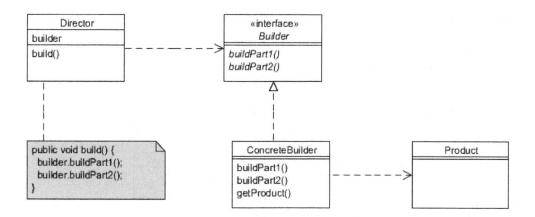

• Builder defines an interface for creating parts of a 'product' object;

• ConcreteBuilder creates and assembles the 'product' parts step-by-step and provides a method to retrieve it during or after assembly;

• Director controls the actual assembly process.

Chain of Responsibility

Type	Behavioural
Purpose	Avoid coupling the sender of a request to its receiver by giving more than one object a chance to handle the request. Chain the receiving objects and pass the request along the chain until an object handles it.
Example usage	When more than one object can handle a request and the handler is not known in advance.
Consequences	Not every request needs to be handled, or maybe it needs to be handled by more than one handler.

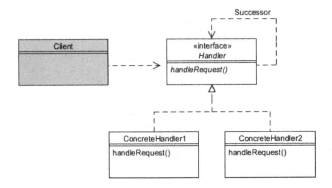

• `Handler` defines an interface for handling requests;

• `ConcreteHandler1` and `ConcreteHandler2` each decide if they can handle the request itself or if it should be passed on to its successor.

Client programs send their requests to the first object in the chain.

Command

Type	Behavioural
Purpose	Encapsulate a request as an object, thereby letting you parameterise clients with different requests, queue or log requests, and support undoable operations.
Example usage	UI controls such as menu items and toolbar buttons. Undo/redo mechanisms.
Consequences	Strive to keep separate the objects that invoke the operation from the object that performs it.

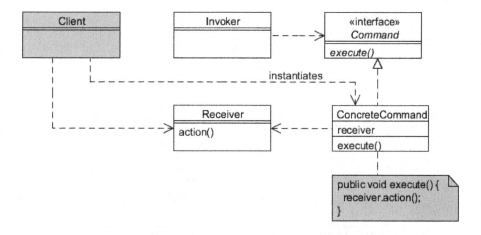

- Command is the interface for executing an operation;

- ConcreteCommand performs the operation on the Receiver;

- Invoker asks the command to be carried out;

- Receiver knows how to perform the operations.

Composite

Type	Structural
Purpose	Compose objects into tree structures to represent part-whole hierarchies. Composite lets clients treat individual objects and compositions of objects uniformly.
Example usage	Graphical component hierarchies, etc.
Consequences	Simple objects can be combined into complex assemblies and all treated through a common interface. Adding new components should be straightforward.

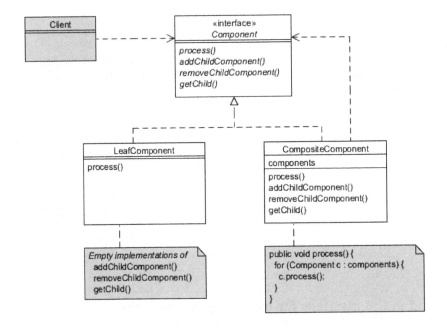

- Component is the interface for both leaves and composites;

- LeafComponent defines objects that have no children;

- CompositeComponent defines objects that may have children.

Decorator

Type	Structural
Purpose	Attach additional responsibilities to an object dynamically. Decorators provide a flexible alternative to subclassing for extending functionality.
Example usage	GUI toolkits file and object input/output streams (e.g. buffering).
Consequences	Can be more flexible than direct inheritance and reduce number of classes required.

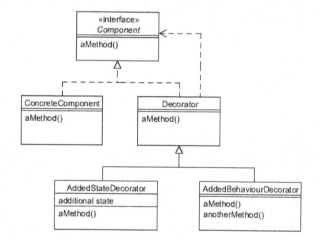

- Component defines the interface for objects that can have responsibilities added to them dynamically;

- ConcreteComponent implements the Component interface;

- Decorator maintains a reference to a Component object as well as defining an interface that matches that of Component;

- AddedStateDecorator and AddedBehaviourDecorator each decorate a Component by adding additional instance variables and/or methods.

Facade

Type	Structural
Purpose	Provide a unified interface to a set of interfaces in a subsystem. Facade defines a higher-level interface that makes the subsystem easier to use.
Example usage	To simplify access to several objects through a single 'facade' object.
Consequences	Needs a new class to be created to serve as the 'facade'.

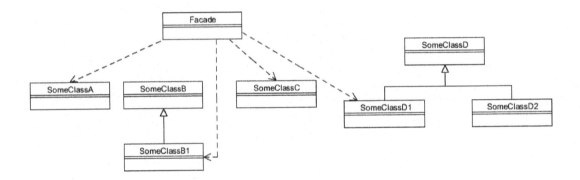

- **Facade** defines the class that provides the simplified interface to other classes;

- SomeClassA, *etc.* are various classes, related or not.

Factory Method

Type	Creational
Purpose	Define an interface for creating an object, but let subclasses decide which class to instantiate.
Example usage	When you can't anticipate the specific type of object to be created, or you want to localise the knowledge of which class gets created.
Consequences	Reduces the need for clients to use 'new' to instantiate objects.

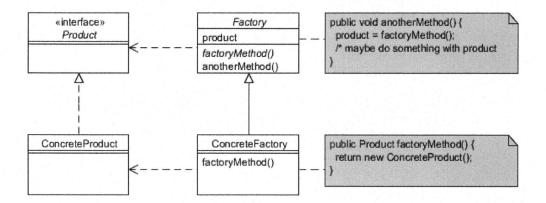

• `Product` defines the interface of the product that is to be created;

• `ConcreteProduct` is an implementation of a particular product;

• `Factory` declares the factory method that returns a `Product` object;

• `ConcreteFactory` implements the factory method defined in `Factory` to return an instance of `Product`.

Flyweight

Type	Structural
Purpose	Use sharing to support large numbers of fine-grained objects efficiently.
Example usage	Text/graphic editors, etc.
Consequences	Saves memory through sharing shared state.

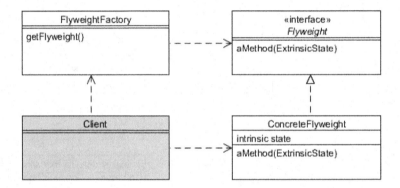

• `Flyweight` defines the interface through which flyweight objects can act on extrinsic state;

• `ConcreteFlyweight` implements `Flyweight` and stores intrinsic state. Must be shareable;

• `FlyweightFactory` creates and manages the flyweight objects through a 'pooling' mechanism.

Client programs maintain references to the flyweights obtained through the factory.

Interpreter

Type	Behavioural
Purpose	Given a language, define a representation for its grammar along with an interpreter that uses the representation to interpret sentences in the language.
Example usage	Simple grammars and mini-language processing.
Consequences	Not suitable for complex grammars and language processing.

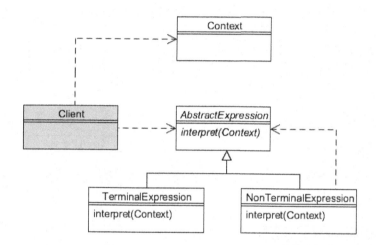

• `AbstractExpression` defines the abstract method to interpret an element;

• `TerminalExpression` extends `AbstractExpression` for language elements that terminate an expression;

• `NonTerminalExpression` extends `AbstractExpression` for language elements that are just part of an expression;

• `Context` is the object that is being parsed (e.g. the grammar or language).

Iterator

Type	Behavioural
Purpose	Provide a way to access the elements of an aggregate object sequentially without exposing its underlying representation.
Example usage	Wherever a collection or array of objects or values need to be processed in turn.
Consequences	The for-each syntax simplifies usage.

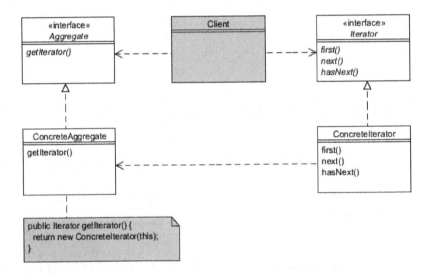

- Iterator defines the interface for the iterator;

- ConcreteIterator implements Iterator to perform the processing of each element in Aggregate;

- Aggregate defines the interface for the collection to be processed;

- ConcreteAggregate implements Aggregate for the actual collection.

Mediator

Type	Behavioural
Purpose	Define an object that encapsulates how a set of objects interact. Mediator promotes loose coupling by keeping objects from referring to each other explicitly, and it lets you vary their interaction independently.
Example usage	Dialogs that control UI components, etc.
Consequences	The Mediator could be defined to use the Observer pattern to monitor the components.

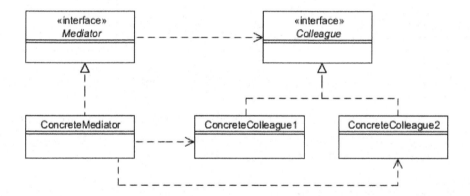

• `Mediator` defines the interface for communication with `Colleague` objects;

• `ConcreteMediator` implements the `Mediator` interface and performs the communication;

• `Colleague` defines the interface for a component that needs communication with the `Mediator`;

• `ConcreteColleague1` and `ConcreteColleague2` implement the `Colleague` interface and performs the communication with the `Mediator` such that it needs no knowledge of any other `Colleague`.

Memento

Type	Behavioural
Purpose	Without violating encapsulation, capture and externalise an object's internal state so that it can be restored to this state later.
Example usage	Undo & Redo processing, database transactions, etc.
Consequences	Encapsulates the storage of state external to the originating object, but might be expensive in terms of memory or performance.

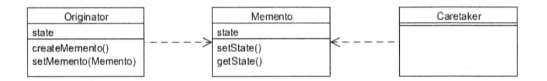

- Originator creates the Memento object and uses it to restore its state;

- Memento stores the state of Originator;

- Caretaker keeps the memento.

Observer

Type	Behavioural
Purpose	Define a one-to-many dependency between objects so that when one object changes its state, all its dependants are notified and updated automatically.
Example usage	GUI controls, events, etc.
Consequences	Decouples classes through a common interface.

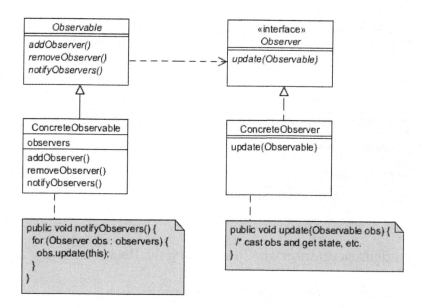

- Observable defines the mechanisms to register observers and notify them of events;

- ConcreteObservable extends Observable for a particular subject class;

- Observer defines an interface for interested classes;

- ConcreteObserver implements Observer for a particular interested class.

Prototype

Type	Creational
Purpose	Specify the kinds of objects to create using a prototypical instance, and create new objects by copying the prototype.
Example usage	Where easier or faster to clone than to instantiate.
Consequences	Cloning might become difficult in certain situations

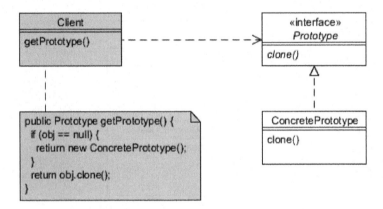

- Prototype defines an interface that can 'clone' itself;

- ConcretePrototype performs the self-cloning.

Client programs create new objects by asking a prototype to clone itself.

Proxy

Type	Structural
Purpose	Provide a surrogate or place-holder for another object to control access to it.
Example usage	Java RMI, security proxies, etc.
Consequences	RMI runs on multiple JVMs.

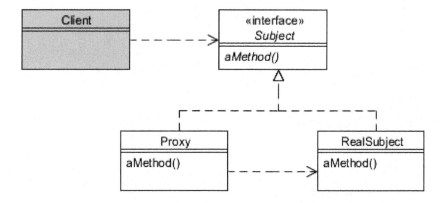

- `Subject` defines the interface that needs to be accessed through a proxy;

- `RealSubject` defines the actual object which `Proxy` represents;

- `Proxy` maintains a reference to `RealSubject` so it can act on its behalf.

Singleton

Type	Creational
Purpose	Ensure a class allows only one object to be created, providing a single point of access to it.
Example usage	Log files, configuration settings, etc.
Consequences	Often overused, difficult to subclass, can lead to tight coupling.

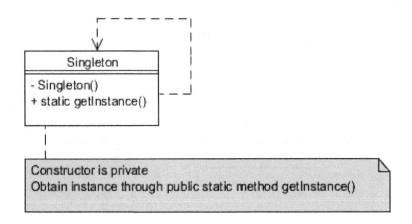

• `Singleton` defines a `private` constructor together with a `public` class (i.e. `static`) method as the only means of getting the instance.

Note that this book recommends using an `enum` to implement the *Singleton* pattern in most instances.

State

Type	Behavioural
Purpose	Allow an object to alter its behaviour when its internal state changes. The object will appear to change its class.
Example usage	UI shape components, etc.
Consequences	Localises state-specific behaviour and separates behaviour for different states.

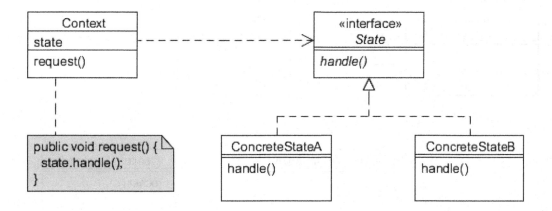

• `State` defines the interface for handling different states in the `handle()` method;

• `ConcreteStateA` and `ConcreteStateB` implement the `State` interface for each separate state;

• `Context` holds a reference to a `State` object to request a particular state.

Strategy

Type	Behavioural
Purpose	Define a family of algorithms, encapsulate each one, and make them interchangeable. Strategy lets the algorithm vary independently from clients that use it.
Example usage	Java Swing borders.
Consequences	Might need to pass data to each strategy.

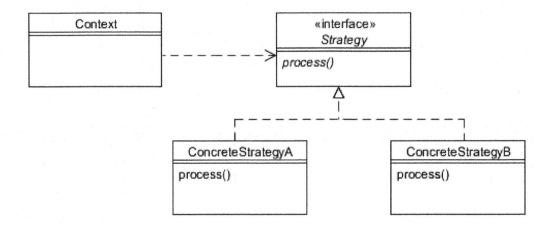

- Strategy defines the interface for the algorithms;

- ConcreteStrategyA and ConcreteStrategyB implement Strategy for a particular algorithm;

- Context holds a reference to the Strategy that is being used.

Template Method

Type	Behavioural
Purpose	Define the skeleton of an algorithm in a method, deferring some steps to subclasses. Template Method lets subclasses redefine certain steps of an algorithm without changing the algorithm's structure.
Example usage	When an algorithm's steps can be performed in different ways.
Consequences	Should prevent the template method from being overridden.

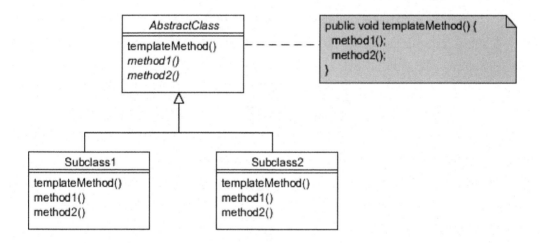

• `AbstractClass` defines the non-overridable `templateMethod()` that invokes a series of abstract methods defined in subclasses;

• `Subclass1` and `Subclass2` extend `AbstractClass` to define the code for each abstract method invoked by `templateMethod()`.

Visitor

Type	Behavioural
Purpose	Represent a method to be performed on the elements of an object structure. Visitor lets you define a new method without changing the classes of the elements on which it operates.
Example usage	Similar operations need performing on different types in a structure, or as a means to add functionality without extensive modifications.
Consequences	Adding new visitable objects can require modifying visitors.

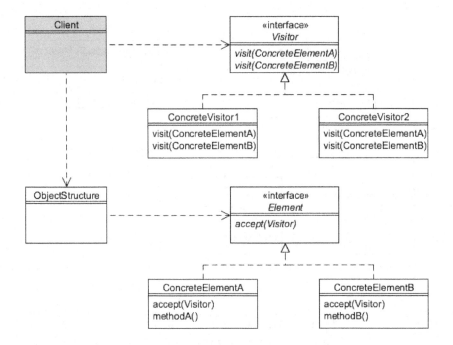

• `Visitor` defines the interface that declares methods to visit each kind of visitable `Element`;

• `ConcreteVisitor1` and `ConcreteVisitor2` implement the `Visitor` interface for each element that could be visited;

• `Element` defines the interface for all classes which could be visited;

- `ConcreteElementA` and `ConcreteElementB` implement the `Element` interface for each class that could be visited.

- `ObjectStructure` contains references to all objects that can be visited, enabling iteration through them.

Appendix C. Bibliography

Beck, Kent. *Extreme programming explained; Embrace Change.* Reading, MA: Addison-Wesley, 1999.

Bevis, Tony. *Java programming step-by-step.* Essex, UK: Ability First Limited, 2012.

Bloch, Joshua. *Effective Java: programming language guide.* River, NJ: Addison-Wesley, 2001.

Cooper, James W. *Java design patterns: a tutorial.* Reading, MA: Addison-Wesley, 2000.

Court, Lindsey, et al. *Software development with Java.* Milton Keynes, The Open University, 2007.

Fowler, Martin, et al. *Refactoring: improving the design of existing code.* River, NJ: Addison-Wesley, 2000.

Fowler, Martin, and Kendall Scott. *UML distilled, second edition: a brief guide to the standard object modeling language.* River, NJ: Addison-Wesley, 1999.

Freeman, Eric, et al. *Head first design patterns.* Sebastopol, CA : O'Reilly, 2004.

Gamma, Erich, et al. *Design patterns: elements of reusable object-oriented software.* River, NJ: Addison-Wesley, 1995.

Gilbert, Stephen, and Bill McCarty. *Object-oriented design in java.* Corte Madera, CA: Waite Group Press, 1998.

Laney, Robin, et al. *Software engineering with objects.* Milton Keynes, The Open University, 2008.

Langr, Jeff. *Java style: patterns for implementation.* River, NJ: Prentice-Hall PTR, 2000.

Index

Also available

Java Programming Step-by-Step is suitable both for beginners and those with some programming experience. This book will guide you step-by-step through the development of a desktop application written using the Java programming language. No prior knowledge is assumed, and each step is clearly explained so you can follow along in your own time.

ISBN 978-0-9565758-2-1

Coverage includes:

- How to apply essential object-oriented concepts;
- How to define classes, interfaces, variables & methods;
- How to use conditional statements, arrays, loops and sorts;
- How to structure your application to make it easy to write, enhance and maintain;
- How to properly document, test and debug your programs;
- How to define and use events, listeners and exceptions;
- How to use threads to make your program run more than one process as the same time;
- How to design and develop a user-friendly graphical user interface using buttons, labels, text fields, drop-down selectors, checkboxes, radio buttons, sliders, menu-bars, icon toolbars, etc.
- How to save your program's data to a disk file.

Available from Amazon USA, UK and worldwide.

For more information visit: www.abilityfirst.co.uk/books

CPSIA information can be obtained at www.ICGtesting.com
Printed in the USA
LVOW03s1018301014

411241LV00004B/27/P